Violence and Law in the Modern Age

Violence and Law in the Modern Age

ANTONIO CASSESE

Translated by S.J.K. Greenleaves

Princeton University Press

Princeton, New Jersey

First published in the English language 1988 by Princeton University Press,
41 William Street, Princeton, New Jersey 08540

Library of Congress Cataloging in Publication Data

Cassese, Antonio.
  [Violenza e diritto nell'era nucleare. English]
  Violence and law in the modern age / Antonio Cassese.
      p.   cm.
  Translation of: Violenza e diritto nell'era nucleare.
  Bibliography: p.
  Includes index.
  ISBN 0-691-07783-5 (alk. paper) :
  1. Nuclear arms control–History. I. Title.
JX1974.7.C35413   1988   88–3642
327.1′74′09–dc19

Printed in Great Britain

Contents

Introduction

In that remarkable work of mediation between two cultures, *De l'Allemagne* (1813), Mme de Staël recounted an anecdote: a tutor remarked to a prince who wished to study mathematics, and had become impatient with the diligence and hours of study required by such a rigorous subject, that the diligence and study were necessary, 'because there is no royal way for mathematics' (*il n'y a point de route royale en mathématiques*).[1] Mme de Staël then warned her French public, 'which has many reasons for considering itself a prince', that there is no royal way leading to metaphysics either; she went on to explain the main points of Kantian philosophy with her usual clarity.

This anecdote has haunted my thoughts more than once in recent years. Since it is part of my job to peruse diplomatic dispatches and international treaties that often lie gathering dust on their shelves, and thumb through the documents and resolutions of international organizations, I could not help but apply Mme de Staël's expression to my own subject. Thus, I have often wondered whether there was, if not a 'royal way', at least some other means of transmitting certain international problems from the remote lecture rooms of universities and from the halls of dry academic discussion to the wider audiences of those who follow the ups and downs of international affairs with passionate interest. My intention is not so much to popularize the subject as to involve the general public in a debate that often takes place, alas, only among a handful of experts.

The *coup de grâce*, so to speak, came in 1979. I had been turning these ideas over in my mind for quite some time, but

that year, thanks to Arnaldo Momigliano, I 'discovered' Moses
Finley. (One evening, while we were walking through the
streets of Oxford between showers, discussing American con-
tributions to British culture, Momigliano told me about Finley,
who, having sought refuge in Cambridge from the McCarthy
persecutions of the 1950s, had found in Great Britain a
congenial climate for his determination to 'revive' the ancient
world.) After reading Finley's work, what struck me most was
not so much his effort to speak to an educated public as a whole
(a typical feature of Anglo-Saxon culture in general) as his skill
in bringing into focus the social, political and cultural problems
of the ancient world that still contain a message for us today. I
was also intrigued by the method he had chosen: in line with
the canons of the Frankfurt School he looked at single aspects
of Graeco-Roman life as parts of the whole; in each individual
problem he always tried to discover the presence and incidence
of the whole socio-political context.

After passionately reading my way through Finley's works,
with due humility I decided to try out his method in my own
field of interest. I thus turned my attention to certain Gordian
knots of international affairs, intending to show how the
various elements – political, economic, ideological and juridical
– all interact in the sphere of interstate relations. Not unwitting-
ly I chose to examine issues with a tenuous legal import: issues
involving relations of force between the Great Powers, or
between them and lesser states, and which are concerned
primarily with ideology and with political and military necessity, while leaving legal imperatives to one side. In tackling
these issues, I hoped to show how legal rules either have or
could have a say even in the case of 'major problems'. (It goes
without saying that these rules play a vital role in day-to-day
relations – commercial, economic and others – in which,
conversely, the politico-ideological, politico-military
component is less obtrusive.)

I have preferred to lay my cards on the table and, however
brazen they may seem, to declare my intentions in writing this
book with all possible frankness. I hope it will be clear to the
reader that I have not sought a 'royal way' to the international
political and juridical reality. With one eye on those who are
interested in international affairs, whether as experts or lay-
men, I have tried to discuss certain important themes that, in

my opinion, should make us all sit up and think, and on which any new voice, however discordant, is always welcome. It is up to the reader to decide whether, and to what extent, I have failed to achieve my aim.

I feel it is useful to emphasize two or three central ideas that underlie these pages and are their leitmotifs.

The first is that, after the Second World War, relations and tensions between the two opposite poles of 'force' and 'law' changed, to a certain extent, in the international community (as well as within the systems of single states). Two macroscopic events – both sinister and dramatic – marked this change: the genocide of the Jewish people and the atomic bombs dropped on Japan. One should not think however that the world awoke one morning filled with greater evil than ever before. The two events have acquired a tragically new meaning, both from a quantitative and qualitative point of view, because of precise historical circumstances. With the wholesale massacre of the Jews, the traditional pogrom took a leap forward thanks to the advent of the totalitarian state. The old anti-Semitic feelings, which once led to 'spontaneous' massacre, became the object of political directives issued by government officials and put into operation by an orderly and efficient bureaucratic machinery. The occasional explosion of mass homicidal violence was transformed into a bureaucratic plan, carefully and minutely laid by thousands of civil servants working without the intermediate action of pressure groups or political associations that could oppose or mediate the directives as they passed from the national leader and the state apparatus to the state community. In the case of Hiroshima and Nagasaki, unpredictable advances in modern science, and their ever-increasing application by government bodies in the 'pathological' context of a war to be fought to the bitter end, are the premise and background to the use of an instrument of death that has subverted everything, or almost everything, in international relations.

These two events have dramatized and exasperated the tension between the two poles of 'force' and 'law', or, in Camus' terms, between 'bullets' and 'words' (*les balles et les paroles*).[2] Violence has increased disproportionately. The massacre of the Jews and the extermination of so many civilians in the two Japanese towns reveal to what extent state apparatuses feel free to use violence. We know that a force one hundred times greater is now in the hands of at least some of the Great Powers, making them capable of destroying the world instantly and several times over. However, violence is used in a thousand less macroscopic and more 'commonplace' forms: these include acts of genocide, murderous civil strife which bespatters the world, terrorist attacks which receive greater or lesser 'official' sanction and wars between states in which neither side balks at using barbarous means of destruction such as chemical weapons and napalm, nor shies away from slaughtering the enemy's civilian population. A sovereign state is now free to use extreme forms of violence that were once unthinkable, not only against its own citizens but against the peoples of other nations – whether directly or through the indirect medium of terrorist groups.

As 'force' made giant strides, so 'law' tried to keep abreast. Single laws have tried to turn aside the sword. Not only has a new world organization been set up, the United Nations, which its founders hoped would prevent a repetition of the 'Great New Fact' (an expression Churchill coined in speaking of the atomic bomb).[3] But legal rules have also been devised to help curb the new violence. However, pressure from conflicting economic and military interests and the clash of antagonistic ideologies has prevented this 'new' law from shaping the actions of states. Today, 'classic' or traditional law, which was realistic (because it faithfully reflected the balance of power among subjects of the international community), has been overlaid by 'idealistic' law: a set of rules and institutions that, to a large extent, reflect the need to transform relations as they now stand and proclaim a duty to do more than merely consecrate things as they are. Besides these tender, fragile new precepts, there is what B.V.A. Röling, the great Dutch international lawyer, called the 'natural law of the nuclear age',[4] that is to say all those ethical and political imperatives sanctioned by UN resolutions and by resolutions from other international forums; these are imperatives that the Third World hopes to use to upset (or at least modify) the existing order, by introducing principles of international economic justice and by demanding that the enormous resources used today in the arms race should be devolved on poor countries to help them develop. The tug-of-war between 'force' and 'law', which previously played a covert and unobtrusive role in the international community (precisely because law merely endorsed force), *has now begun in earnest.*

The second fundamental concept underpinning my analysis is that it would be a great mistake to refuse to examine the relations that exist between these two poles in a nuclear age: such a refusal would be based on the premise that states, those 'cold monsters' without souls, never listen to the voice of 'law' since they are moved only by *motivations of 'power' and 'force'*. In my opinion, this premise is false. On closer examination, it is not true that, when their essential military, economic and political interests are at stake, states trifle with the Tables of the Law (all things considered, Dean Acheson was alone in saying, apropos the Cuban crisis,that 'law simply does not deal with such questions of ultimate power – power that comes close to the sources of sovereignty')[5]. Their strategy is more subtle than simply transgressing the legal 'commandments'. It consists in preventing their legal crystallization, or – if the pressure of public opinion makes this impossible – in wording them in terms as ambiguous as possible. By so doing, they can then interpret these legal standards as best they please, adapting them to the requirements of the moment and bending them to their contingent interests. If we thumb through the records of the last forty or fifty years, we can easily see that no state, great or small, has ever admitted to breaking the commonly accepted legal canons. (Take, for example, the ban on chemical warfare, or on weapons that cause unnecessary suffering; the ban on indiscriminate attacks on undefended towns, or, on a larger scale, on acts of genocide, and so on.) Whenever they are accused of violating these and other no less important international rules, states immediately make denials, or else they point to the exceptional circumstances which they feel legitimize their course of action; or they say that the international rules prohibit not their own but other forms of behaviour. Recently, the South African government went so far as to assert that it was as much against racial discrimination as all the other nations of the world; however, the government felt that the 'distinctions' based on the colour of a person's skin, as practised in South Africa, are not forms of racial segregation, but are only intended to encourage the separate development of different human communities.

Since states behave in this manner, it would be useful to understand whether certain international rules have been formed and, if so, what loopholes there are. In this way one might try to tighten the meshes of the 'legal network' that surrounds them, reducing their room for manoeuvre by criticism and new proposals.

This leads me to my third general concept. What *attitude* should be adopted by *jurists* – but also, more generally, by all those who are involved in international affairs – *vis-à-vis* 'positive law'? In my opinion, the scepticism of 'traditionalists' and 'realists' is groundless. After all, where does it lead? It leads to a position of never questioning the role of 'force' in international affairs. Jurists who behave in this manner, with the approval of most politicians and diplomats, and accuse their fellows of being artless Johnny Head-in-Airs, not only misunderstand how states behave (a point on which I have already dwelt), but cripple their own role. They enthusiastically force themselves into a straight-jacket; they decline to look beyond the railings that enclose positive law: not only do they refuse to entertain doubts about existing law, they also turn their backs on those areas in which law is, for reasons I have already mentioned, uncertain and 'magmatic'. These jurists belong to the ranks of those who Kant – speaking of Grotius, Pufendorf, Vattel and others who used legal arguments to justify the waging of war – described as 'irritating comforters' (*leidige Tröster*).[6] Feeling quite safe behind a veritable stockade of positivist doctrine, they prefer the solid ground of what the law dictates, where they build airy conceptual castles whose irrelevance for society they occasionally perceive. (I once asked one of these sophisticated jurists what made him engrave such refined conceptual structures. In answer he told me the story of a medieval sculptor who was asked by a passing knight why he took such pains to polish a statuette that stood on a high pinnacle of the cathedral and could not be clearly seen from below; his reply was: 'I am working for the angels'.) These jurists, together with the politicans and diplomats who share their ideas, have not understood one important point. Sovereign states are undoubtedly mighty machines powered by 'nationalistic interest'. However, as we daily observe, there is a conflict of forces within the state apparatus, some championing needs that are not those of *realpolitik*. There is no lack of foreign ministers ready to promote progressive and humanitarian issues!

One decisive factor assists these progressive forces: public opinion, both at home and abroad. In the past, states have frequently been forced to act under the pressure of public opinion (or at least have claimed it was among their motivations). Let me quote one of many such examples: in 1915, when the Ottoman Empire started the persecution and genocide of the Armenians, Germany protested, saying that 'she [felt] all the more obliged to draw the Ottoman Empire's attention to this fact because public opinion already [tended] to believe that Germany, as Turkey's friend and ally, [may have] approved or even instigated those acts of violence.'[7] The role of public opinion has grown over the years. Thus in 1931 the eminent English jurist J.L. Brierly noted that within the state a breach of law can go unnoticed and, in any case, when it is noticed, the transgressor is often indifferent to 'social stigma'; on the other hand, in the international community it is almost impossible for states to perpetrate grave violations of hallowed standards of conduct and escape public disapproval, and besides, states are necessarily very sensitive to public censure. Today, the growing power of the press and of the mass media generally has greatly increased the importance of public opinion, especially in democratic countries. But even states in which the media is manipulated by government authorities cannot ignore the repercussions of their political, military and economic action on the opinion of foreign governments, promptly alerted by the various (often Western) channels of information.

By relying on these forces, as well as on many non-governmental organizations which are more and more committed and pugnacious, there is hope that something may yet be achieved. By acting on the 'twilight' area in which violations prevail and law seems to dissolve into air, jurists, and all those who are involved in the conduct of state affairs, can be of some use to the voices of dissent and, above all, to those who have been, or may in future be, the victims of violence.

1

Hiroshima, Nagasaki and the Imperatives of the International Community

Did the United States violate the international legal rules?

Many people may feel it is futile to wonder whether or not the barbarous bombings of 6 and 9 August 1945 were forbidden by international law. What, they would argue, is the point of asking such a question since, if the bombing was indeed unlawful, no one has yet punished or ever will punish those responsible? Others may object that as a general rule international law, already so fragile in normal circumstances, is bound to be disregarded when it confronts the vital interests of the Great Powers. This being so, why waste time in questions that can only receive 'academic' answers?

Undoubtedly, these objections carry conviction. Yet, the desire to assess facts and human behaviour and judge whether or not they were permissible is deeply rooted: we all feel the need for a decalogue, not only to guide us in our own actions, but to help us judge the actions of others. Now, it is not enough to determine the rights and wrongs of human behaviour in the light of moral tenets. We may question whether acts that seem obviously inadmissible according to our moral beliefs are equally so in the light of other principles. In the case before us, these are principles that have the merit of having been adopted by states and are therefore extrinsic and not personal principles; they bear the seal of approval of all the sovereign entities that make up the international community.

Another reason, I feel, that justifies my question is that those who authorised the dropping of atomic bombs on the Japanese towns and those who were subjected to the bombs asked this very question (though, naturally the answers they gave were very different). In other words, even in exceptionally dramatic circumstances, politicians, statesmen and even the military wonder whether their own actions and those of others are permitted by the rules of behaviour that govern the international community.

Lastly, it is always worth inquiring into cases where the Great Powers have used force with a heavy hand and wondering to what extent their behaviour is sanctioned by contemporary legal imperatives. Such an inquiry can help to throw new light on the nature and limitations of those legal rules and also help to reveal the real motives behind the actions of states.

The facts

Before selecting the rules that can help us to judge the dropping of the atomic bombs, let us examine the 'facts'. It is a formidable task, not because they are little known or because we lack eyewitness accounts and proof of what happened, but because in this case the facts – like other macroscopic atrocities in our time: the genocide of the Jews, racial segregation in South Africa, and so on – are so inhuman that it is repugnant to describe them.

We all know the main features of the atomic bomb. Whereas conventional bombs, however potent, produce two effects (one physical: the air is shifted so violently that buildings and bridges collapse, and so on; the other caloric: a wave of heat provokes fires), the atomic bomb produces a third effect: radioactivity. As soon as the neutrons and gamma rays hit a human being they destroy cells and, if they do not kill, they weaken the body and cause leukaemia and other very serious illnesses.

These were the effects produced by the two bombs dropped on 6 and 9 August 1945 on the two Japanese towns which, according to Japanese estimates, contained 336,000 and 270,000 people respectively. All survivors agree on the sequence of events: first a great flash, as of magnesium, then a wave of heat and then a terrible explosion. Almost all the buildings were razed to the ground and fires broke out everywhere among the rubble. Then it began to rain great, black, greasy raindrops (bomb splinters, scattered throughout

the air in the form of particles clinging to drops of water, caused
this radioactive rain). The official reports on the victims are also
well known. The (conservative) estimates produced by the
Japanese government during the 1950s (at a trial in Tokyo, to
which I shall return later) gave 78,000 dead and 51,000 wounded
out of 336,000 for Hiroshima and 23,000 dead and 41,000
wounded out of 270,000 for Nagasaki. But it is not the number of
victims that makes the bombings stand out (indeed, many
writers have pointed out that more people died in bombing raids
with conventional weapons, in Tokyo or in other Japanese cities,
as well as in such European cities as Dresden and Nuremberg).
What distinguishes Hiroshima and Nagasaki is the *quality of
suffering caused* (if we can use such an expression for something
that touches our feelings so deeply). This 'quality' does not
emerge from the figures and statistics (which quantify human
suffering in abstract numbers), but from the accounts of
survivors. Let us now listen to some of these voices and try to
understand what really happened on 6 and 9 August 1945.

A general picture of the effects of the explosion on Hiroshima is given by the German Jesuit, Father John Siemes, who
was two kilometres away from the city in the Jesuit novitiate:

As a result of the explosion of the bomb at 8:15[August 6] almost the
entire city was destroyed at a single blow. Only small outlying districts
in the southern and eastern parts of the town escaped complete
destruction. The bomb exploded over the centre of the city. As a result
of the blast, the small Japanese houses in a diameter of five kilometers,
which comprised 99% of the city, collapsed or were blown up. Those
who were in the houses were buried in the ruins. Those who were in the
open sustained burns resulting from contact with the substance or rays
emitted by the bomb. Where the substance struck in quantity, fires
sprang up. These spread rapidly.

The heat which rose from the centre created a whirlwind which was
effective in spreading fire throughout the whole city. Those who had
been caught beneath the ruins and who could not be freed rapidly, and
those who had been caught by the flames, became casualties. As much
as six kilometers from the centre of the explosion, all houses were
damaged and many collapsed and caught fire. Even fifteen kilometers
away, windows were broken.[1]

The following day the scene was terrifying: 'Where the city
stood, everything as far as the eye can reach, is a waste of ashes

and ruin.'[2] Twenty days later the delegate from the International Committee of the Red Cross, F. Bilfinger, described Hiroshima as follows in a telegram to the Red Cross in Tokyo: 'Horrifying situation . . . Indescribable conditions. Effects of bomb mysteriously serious.'[3]

The colossal destruction affected not only the soldiers (in the words of Father Siemes: 'especially hard hit were the soldiers. The Pioneer Regiment was almost entirely wiped out. The barracks were near the centre of the explosion')[4], but civilians. No doubt this also happened when conventional weapons were used in bombing raids. The 'conventional' bombing was also decidedly contrary to the rules in force at the time, as it would be today, but this serves merely to emphasize that there was no great difference, from this point of view, between the use of atomic bombs and the way conventional bombs were often used during the Second World War.

Here is part of the eyewitness account of a woman, Satoko Matsumoto, who was among the survivors in Hiroshima:[5]

Last night the sirens had gone off several times and I was now all covered in sweat after running from my home to the shelter and back; I needed a wash. I found a bar of kitchen soap . . . had a bath and started to wash my head. But some soap got in my eyes and I could not see, when a most violent flash lit up everything around me . . . I picked up my little girl (who was two) . . . As I took her up, the house collapsed and we were buried under the rubble. My first struggles brought more plaster down on our heads. Finally, I managed to free myself and the baby and, with great care, clambered out into the open. But then I stood amazed: all the buildings in the town seemed to have been razed to the ground and nothing vertical was left standing to testify to the familiar surroundings that had been there a few minutes earlier. Mount Eba, which I had never been able to see from my home, now appeared before my eyes. Among the clouds of dust and smoke I could make out human silhouettes moving east towards us. The roads were buried under the rubble and the people were picking their way over the ruins. Some were quite naked; others only wore trousers. Very few had managed to bring away anything. At first I thought that some were dressed in rags, but then I realized that it was their skin peeling off, leaving the flesh naked . . .

Then it began to rain. Great drops fell on the naked flesh of those burnt figures. Mad with pain, they ran to the nearby fields to shelter under any vegetation they could find. But I noticed at once something strange: this rain-water was neither transparent nor refreshing; it was dark, thick and gummy like kerosene. It stuck to my hair and my skin, which were already covered in red dust from the rubble of my house . . .

My father had been wounded, apparently only slightly. But he soon showed symptoms of radiation, when one's skin is covered in red spots. His was truly a form of martyrdom and, on the evening of 22 August, after wandering into the fields to forget his suffering, he fell down dead.

In the words of one of the survivors from Nagasaki:

Confused and terrified, I began to run towards the hills where there were strong shelters. The roads were choked with a flood of survivors. Some, with their skin hanging in shreds like rags and so burnt that one could not tell men from women, were asking for help. They ran in every direction with only one idea in their heads: to escape.

Very similar is the eyewitness account of Tsugiya Umebayashi, who was ten when the bomb fell. This is how she described her flight from Nagasaki:

Our compartment on the train was full of refugees. The air stank with their sores, on which flies settled obstinately despite all efforts to shoo them off; many wounds were gangrenous. Some spat blood into the wash basin. Others were completely bald. It was impossible to tell men from women.

All accounts agree not only on the intense suffering of the wounded and the dying, but also on their *astonishment* and that of their rescuers, because what had occurred was beyond the bounds of the imaginable. One survivor from Hiroshima, Kazuo Matsumuro, after describing his miraculous escape, spoke of the other wounded as follows:

From time to time from that veritable wall of fire created by the flames, half naked men emerged covered in blood; other ghosts like these hurried in search of shelter. Some had been exposed to tremendous radiation from the bomb and their skin was peeling off and hung from their nails when they held out their hands. Their monstrous wounds revealed raw flesh from which blood flowed. But no one was crying out: such was their astonishment that they could neither weep nor moan.

The feeling of astonishment for the incommensurable and extraordinary nature of the tragedy helps to explain how surprised and impotent the rescuers felt. Tatsuko Mori, a survivor from Hiroshima, said: 'No one knew how to treat those wounds, nobody had ever seen their like before and we all felt aghast and disgusted and could not imagine the reason for this sudden and inexplicable tragedy.' The same attitude was to be found among the official relief corps; in the words of a nurse from Hiroshima, seriously wounded herself: 'A military surgeon stood beside me. I asked what I could do, showing him my wounds. He stayed silent for a long time. Then, in a voice of stunned resignation, he said: "No one can do anything. They have dropped something awful; what can it have been?"'

One other aspect of the atomic bombing should not be forgotten. The destruction was so vast it included almost all the hospitals and medical care centres where the wounded might have found help. With respect to Hiroshima, this was one of the points that Father Siemes noted (but he also complained of the Japanese lack of initiative in bringing first aid and their tendency to accept the catastrophe with fatalism, their only worry being to seek out the survivors of their own families).

One of the most inhuman features of the atomic bomb was the long term effects on the bodies of the survivors. John Hersey, writer and journalist, soon noticed this fact after spending a month in Hiroshima in May 1946 writing a special report – later to become famous – on what had happened. 'As if nature were protecting man against his own ingenuity, the reproductive processes were affected for a time; men became sterile, women had miscarriages, menstruation stopped.'[6] The suffering became more acute after a period of months or years. As Kakuji Miyazaki, who worked for the Mitsubishi arms industry in Nagasaki, said:

In 1950 I felt the first symptoms of atomic sickness: my gums began to bleed, I suffered from acute anaemia, from time to time I fainted and fell to the ground in a state of total apathy. The number of my white corpuscles went down rapidly. As soon as I started to work or when I studied at night, my eyes became bloodshot and puffy. The anguish that went with this sickness darkened my everyday life.

The main consequences that appeared after a time were *genetic* – perhaps one of the most horrifying characteristics of radioactivity. Let us listen again to the words of survivors. A man from Hiroshima told how his wife, who was pregnant when the bomb fell, gave birth to a little girl in February 1946:

> The Ministry of Health and Welfare called the sickness with which she (the child) was affected 'syndrome caused by close exposure to radiation at the start of pregnancy'. Microcephalic and mentally retarded, she suffers from many other complications . . . In general the doctors warn the parents that children suffering from this illness never reach the age of twenty. But our daughter is over thirty now. She cannot go to the bathroom alone and her mental age is that of a two-year-old child.

In the account of a survivor from Nagasaki, Toyomi Hashimoto:

> In 1952, four years after his birth, I noticed that my fourth son had an abnormal eye. The opthalmic surgeon diagnosed cancer of the eye, an extremely rare disease that can occur in one case out of ten thousand . . . About fifteen months later, the same child started to cough in a strange manner . . . When I saw that he was getting worse, I took him again to the doctor and learned he had diptheria . . . In June 1956 we had a fifth child; my happiness was short-lived. I had hoped he would replace the child we had lost; instead, by a tragic irony, he had the same eye complaint as his brother. The boy died after an operation.

Legal precepts

My task becomes less distressing when I pass from the 'facts' to the law. Of course, these laws are the offspring of terrible suffering, born only after repeated instances of mass violence and cruelty, when public opinion and a handful of statesmen began to feel that those instances of violence were unacceptable and tried to prohibit, by law, their recurring, in the hope that such legal 'commands' would indeed prevent any repetition. Over the years the underlying suffering has become 'remote', almost as if it had evaporated. The legal rule is a cold, impassive imperative that has forgotten the historical circumstances out of which it came.

In 1945 no rule existed specifically banning the use of the atomic bomb, if only because it was an entirely new weapon. However, two general principles did exist as blanket precepts, adaptable to a wide range of forms of combat. The first principle prohibits the use of any means or method of warfare that can provoke superfluous suffering. The second prohibits the hitting of soldiers and civilians indiscriminately. Although it is easy to draw attention to these principles, it is difficult to give precise account of their scope, that is of what is prohibited and what is permitted. This ambiguity is in no way fortuitous. States are prepared to obey humanitarian imperatives only to a limited extent, especially when they relate to the use of armed force. Since states were forced by public opinion at home and abroad to accept the two precepts and give them solemn expression in international acts, they made sure they were worded in ambiguous terms so as to retain plenty of room for manoeuvre.

Let us take a look at the principle that prohibits the use of arms that cause unnecessary suffering. What pain is superfluous? What pain is necessary? By what yardstick should one measure whether or not the suffering is justified? These are questions to which one can give only partial answers, even after thumbing through diplomatic archives, the chronicles of battles and the declarations of statesmen and diplomats. In my opinion, there is very little that is certain. The principle arose from the *intention* of banning specific weapons: the use of poison and poisoned weapons (as early as the seventeenth century), explosive bullets under 400 grams (1868), dumdum bullets and asphyxiating and toxic gases (1899). It was said at the time that these weapons did not aim only at putting an adversary *hors de combat* (by killing or wounding him) as 'traditional' bullets did, but were meant to cause terrible suffering that could not be justified according to the aim of war: to prevent as many of the enemy as possible from taking part in the hostilities. Let me mention here what the Portuguese government wrote in 1868 to the Tzar of Russia, who had suggested that explosive bullets be banned. Portugal entirely agreed with the proposal and said that the bullets:

> lead to certain death, after appalling suffering, of all those who are hit, often even in cases where other bullets would merely put a soldier *hors de combat*. Consequently, they resemble poisoned bullets, bullets full of glass and lime, and other weapons or means of warfare that cause unnecessary pain, wounds that may never heal, and, according to the most trusty jurists, they have in effect been banned by all civilized nations.[7]

In 1899, at the First Hague Peace Conference, the banning of specific arms that cause superfluous suffering was transformed into a *general principle*, applicable to any means of warfare. This, would be a step towards humanitarian laws of war, as it elevated the merely moral and psychological impulse behind the ban on *specific* weapons into a *general principle*. The advance was however an illusion: the new principle was so vague it could not serve as a sure guide to belligerents; indeed, had it not been expressed in such general terms, it would not have been accepted by the Great Powers, who would never have submitted to a precise, rigorous and wide-ranging ban, for fear of having their hands tied in the future.

In spite of this flaw, the principle was invoked in later years in some cases: for example, on the issues of asphyxiating gases (Ethiopia protested against Italy in 1936) and of conventional weapons such as saw-edged bayonets (the French accusations against the Germans in the First World War), or of bullets of an 'irregular' shape (during the same war the Italians accused the Austrians of using them).[8]

The other principle, banning the indiscriminate use of arms, is no less imprecise. When is the firing of bullets indiscriminate? In certain cases the answer is easy: when, *by its very nature*, the weapon cannot distinguish between civilians and combatants. It is worth recalling here the accusations launched in 1944 by Winston Churchill against Germany in the House of Commons for using the V2s against Britain;[9] these accusations were recognized as legitimate even in the manual of war law (1961) of the Federal Republic of Germany (although the manual, an official document binding on the FRG's troops, does in fact justify the Nazis, because it states that the V2s were launched as a reprisal against the unlawful acts of the Allies).[10] The case is more difficult when the weapon is being used 'discriminately'; that is against the belligerents, and hits civilians as well. This is because when war is waged in the air (aeroplanes hitting objectives on the ground) or on land, the enemy military objectives are rarely isolated and far from the civilian population (this 'ideal' situation only exists in war at sea). Within what limits, therefore, is it legitimate to hit objectives that are both military and civilian? Some people have argued – and lately specific legal rules on the subject have been enacted – that a certain *proportion* must be respected.

But, how should this proportion be measured? Is the killing of one hundred civilians proportionate to the capture of a strategically important building?

This principle is equallly ambiguous; it leaves the belligerents plenty of room to act as they feel the military situation requires. Would it be fair to say that in proclaiming the two principles states were being entirely hypocritical, pretending to accept bans that are not bans because they can be eluded at every step? I have already said that the Great Powers, without whose consent these principles would never have become legal precepts, had every reason to leave them as loose as possible. But, once accepted at a legal level, the precepts become standards of behaviour which, however vague, cannot but be used as such, whatever the political and diplomatic intentions of states. Yet, since they are not very effective, they can be applied only in *exceptional circumstances* when their relevance is undeniable. In other words, although the principles do not carry much weight in the 'ordinary' conduct of war, they become effective in highly pathological and 'dramatic' situations, when the disproportion between what they 'impose' and how one or more of the belligerents behaves, is gigantic. One such extreme and exceptional situation is precisely the dropping of atomic bombs on Hiroshima and Nagasaki.

How did the Allies justify themselves?

Before passing judgement on what happened to the two Japanese towns, let us take a look at what the interested parties said at the time to justify, or criticize, the bombing. I have already hinted that both the Americans and the British, as well as the Japanese, appealed to international rules; the former to justify their decision to use the atomic bomb, the latter to condemn its use. Let us examine the arguments on either side.

The most authoritative justification for using the bomb came, naturally, from President Harry Truman, who gave the order to use it. In his declaration on 9 August, after getting back from the Tripartite Conference at Potsdam (according to his *Memoirs* as well as some notes discovered among his papers in 1980), Truman put forward three arguments. First, the atomic bomb helped to shorten the 'agony of war' and to save the lives of thousands of Americans, who would certainly have died if the war had dragged on. Second, the use of the bomb was justified by the fact that the Japanese had treacherously attacked the United States in Pearl Harbor and had violated the laws of war more than once (especially by maltreating and killing American prisoners); in other words, even though he did not say so explicitly, Truman felt that the bomb was a legitimate form of reprisal (in reaction to violations perpetrated by the other side). Third, Truman had ordered his airmen to hit only 'military bases' (the two towns had a number of military installations) and as far as possible to take measures to avoid killing civilians. One of these measures was a warning given in the Potsdam ultimatum of 27 July 1945, in which the unconditional surrender of Japan was demanded to avoid 'the inevitable and complete destruction of the Japanese armed forces and just as inevitably the utter devastation of the Japanese homeland'. Other measures included the dropping of leaflets over many Japanese cities requesting civilians to leave them.[11]

The same arguments (which, however, skipped the idea of reprisals), with greater technical and historical detail, were advanced by the Secretary of War, Henry L. Stimson, in a famous article published in February 1947 in *Harper's Magazine* (and in a slightly reduced version in the *Bulletin of the Atomic Scientists*). Among other points he noted that, before the bomb was used, US forecasts had predicted that if the war were to continue there would have been over a million victims among the Americans, and many others among the Allies, and even greater losses among the Japanese. Therefore, the deaths in Hiroshima and Nagasaki saved the lives of a vast number of people and this alone, Stimson felt, justified the use of the atomic bomb.[12]

The arguments put forward by Winston Churchill in the House of Commons on 16 August 1945, and later in his *Memoirs*, were fairly similar (as Churchill himself recalled, Britain had given its consent to the use of the bomb; for that very reason the United Kingdom was morally involved in Truman's decision to drop it). However, in addition to these arguments, Churchill also saw two 'merits' in using the bomb. First, a psychological one: 'the Japanese people, whose courage I have always admired, might find in the apparition of this almost supernatural weapon an excuse which would save their honour and release them from their obligation of being killed to the last fighting man'. Second, by dropping the bomb and, consequently, shortening the duration of the war, they had prevented the entry of the Soviet Union into the operations against Japan to hasten its defeat; thus, the Americans remained the sole masters of the area and the future occupiers of the defeated country.[13] I mention these two points made by Churchill because in my opinion they both reveal, the second one especially, why the Americans (and the British) were prepared to use such an extreme measure as a weapon that was new and dangerous and was certain to introduce a radical change in the course of the war. It is worth adding that the fundamental idea in Churchill's mind as to the effect – political, military and psychological – of the bomb on the USSR, was to a certain extent also in the minds of the various American administrators, though from a slightly different point of view. For example, to justify the need to use the atomic bomb against the Japanese, James F. Byrnes (Truman's personal representative on the Interim Committee charged with making recommendations to the President on the use of the bomb, and shortly to become Secretary of State) observed that it would be very difficult to persuade the Russians to retreat from Hungary and Romania and that they would be more tractable if impressed by America's military might; a demonstration of the bomb's potential could impress them.[14]

To go back to Truman, how far were his three arguments correct according to international law? I must say at once that they are all extremely dubious. The first (on the need to save thousands of lives, both for the Allies and the Japanese) can be considered valid from a military or strategic point of view; but, from a legal angle, it is hardly sufficient to justify such a highly destructive act. If Truman's argument were valid, a belligerent could decide on the complete destruction of enemy cities inhabited by civilians, or of precious or vital centres (historic monuments, religious shrines) to make the prosecution of war unbearable for his adversary and force him to capitulate. Similarly, a belligerent could decide to use chemical or bacteriological weapons on a large scale to inflict such a rapid and devastating blow on his enemy as to force him to surrender. International rules on the law of war do not allow such actions. The argument on 'saving lives' is valid only if, to achieve this aim, a weapon whose use is *legally allowed beyond all doubt* is employed to kill a large number of the enemy. Therefore, the argument says nothing about whether it is lawful to use a given weapon. Taken on its own it begs the question.

If the first of Truman's arguments is untenable, neither do the others bear examination. Certainly not the second, because reprisals are allowed only if proportionate to the unlawful acts that provoked them; in our case the lack of proportion is obvious. Besides, this argument can, in a way, be dangerous for those who advance it: indeed, the concept of reprisal implies that the action undertaken is prohibited *per se* and becomes lawful because it is carried out in reaction to the unlawful acts of others. Thus, if one propounds the concept of reprisal, one admits implicitly that the bombing as such was prohibited by law (perhaps this explains why Stimson and Churchill ignored the argument).

Lastly, the argument on 'military objectives' and the various precautions adopted is also open to criticism, for at least three reasons. First, although the two Japanese towns had military bases and installations, they also had very large civilian populations; indeed, the number of civilian dead was very great and certainly out of all proportion to the objective of destroying military targets. Nor can it be said that the death of thousands of civilians was 'proportionate' to the military objective of forcing Japan to capitulate. In fact, the comparison of civilian losses and military advantage should be made with an eye to the *direct and immediate military advantage of a specific attack*, not to the possible general advantage, such as the enemy's capitulation (as I have already noted if this were not so, any warlike act of a profoundly inhuman and destructive nature would become lawful because it was justified by having forced the enemy to surrender).

Second, the precautions taken by the Americans (the dropping of leaflets on 27 July and for several days after until 5 August over many Japanese towns to warn the inhabitants that thay would soon be heavily bombed) cannot justify, even in part, the use of the atomic bomb, because they were so obviously inadequate when compared to the horrific potential danger of the bomb. Let me add that these warnings are seldom heeded by the civilian population. This was exactly the case in the two Japanese towns. It is worth recalling here the words of a survivor from Hiroshima, Chizuko Kijima:

> One day an American aeroplane released some leaflets over Hiroshima. I myself did not read any, but I was told that they warned citizens to flee from the town because the Americans did not want to cause victims among the civilians. Our military police prohibited the reading of those leaflets and ordered people to collect them and hand them over to the authorities: 'This is just another trap that those devilish Americans and those barbarous English want to set us', the police told us. Besides, the order not to read those leaflets was a waste of time: we were so sure of Japan's invincibility that we would never have believed them, even if we had read them.[15]

And now for my third objection, to the supreme 'precaution' of sending the Japanese government an ultimatum. Let me say at once that, from a legal point of view, such an ultimatum cannot legitimize a forbidden warlike act. Indeed, from a historical and diplomatic point of view, the wording of the ultimatum proves that Truman, at least, did not intend to make any concessions to the Japanese and used it merely to salve his conscience. Various sources (including the writings of Stimson and Churchill) prove that there was widespread conviction among the Allies that Japan was ready to capitulate, as long as they could prevent the humiliation of the Emperor, Hirohito, a figure of religious veneration. In a memorandum of 2 July 1945, Stimson suggested that the ultimatum should state that the occupation of Japan would not put an end to its 'constitutional monarchy under her present dynasty'.[16] Even Churchill, at Potsdam, tried to persuade Truman that the ultimatum should somehow save Japanese 'military honour' and give them 'some assurance of their national existence, after they had complied with all the safeguards necessary for the conqueror'. But Truman paid no attention to Stimson and told Churchill bluntly that 'he did not think the Japanese had any military honour after Pearl Harbor'. It is quite impossible to say for certain whether the changes in the ultimatum as suggested by Stimson (and, in rather vaguer terms, by Churchill) would have been decisive. Some people (such as B. V. A. Röling who, as judge at the International Tribunal of Tokyo was able to read all the records of the Japanese Imperial Council) feel the proviso suggested by Stimson would have induced the Japanese

Cabinet and the Emperor to accept a surrender, at least on certain conditions.[17] According to a Japanese diplomat (a member of the delegation sent to Moscow in 1945 to convince Stalin to insist with the Allies on the terms of a surrender) the result would have been the opposite.[18] It is difficult to say where the truth lies. Certainly – as an American historian showed in 1954, after a close examination of the relevant documents – as early as January 1945, the Emperor was ready to put an end to the war and, from June, he was even prepared to renounce power.[19] It is a fact that a few days before the Potsdam Conference (June 1945) the Americans had intercepted and decoded the telegrams between Tokyo and the Japanese Embassy in Moscow, proving that the Japanese knew they had been defeated and were ready to capitulate, the only obstacle being the 'unconditional surrender' that the Allies were demanding, mainly because the person and authority of the Emperor would have been damaged by the 'terms of peace' imposed by the victors. Above all, it is quite certain that when on 10 August (after Hiroshima and Nagasaki) the Japanese decided to surrender as requested in the Allied ultimatum of 26 July, in return for a guarantee on the 'sovereignty of the Emperor', the Allies made no promises but, as Stimson later remarked, they *implicitly recognized the position of the Emperor* by announcing that his powers would be subordinate to the orders of the supreme military commander. Thus, *what had not been conceded by the Allies a few weeks earlier, was granted after the two towns had been razed to the ground.* Would it not have been more logical and more humane to have taken this step before exterminating so many innocent people? Perhaps this is evidence that the real motive for using the atomic bomb was to weaken Stalin's 'bargaining power' – to use Churchill's own words – and exploit what Churchill himself called 'the Great New Fact', the possession of the atomic bomb. The USSR, which declared war on Japan on 8 August 1945, did get most of what had been promised at Yalta, but was not allowed to occupy Japan, which – as we all know – fell under the United States' exclusive sphere of influence.

The official reaction of the Japanese

The Japanese government reacted almost at once to the bombing of Hiroshima. On August 10, after another atomic bomb had been dropped on Nagasaki, it sent the United States a protest via Switzerland (the 'Protecting Power' that kept open the channels of communication between the two belligerents). The Japanese government stated that the atomic bomb was not only contrary to the principles of civilization and humanity, but also violated international law, for two reasons. First, because it had indiscriminately killed a huge number of soldiers and civilians; second, the use of the bomb violated the ban on arms that cause superfluous suffering. On this last point the Japanese government made the following precise observations:

> Since the beginning of the present world war, the Government of the United States has declared repeatedly that the use of poison or other inhumane methods of warfare has been regarded as illegal by the public opinion of civilized countries, and that the United States would not use these methods of warfare unless the other countries used them first. However, the bomb in this case, which the United States used this time, exceeds by far in the indiscriminate and cruel character of its efficiency the poison and other weapons whose use has been prohibited hitherto because of this efficiency.[20]

It is apparent that the Japanese government applied the two traditional principles in an original way. It made a *comparison* between the indiscriminate and cruel effects of some weapons that had been specifically banned by international rules and the effects of the atomic bomb, concluding that the former were greatly inferior to the latter and that, therefore, the atomic bomb was among those weapons that must be regarded as prohibited. This was a most intelligent use of the general principles and specific bans, exploiting them to assess the potential of a *new* weapon.

This approach was later abandoned by Japan and the official American theory was accepted in its lieu.[21] The Japanese volte-face – surprising only if we forget the Americanization of Japan after its defeat – was exposed dramatically at the trial initiated by five survivors from the two towns against the Japanese state, with a view to claiming compensation for the damages they had suffered under the bombardment. They had sued the Japanese state because they felt it had illegally waived the rights and claims of its citizens, including the right to compensation, in its peace treaty with the United States; in their view, since the atomic bombing had been unlawful, the

United States was obliged to pay compensation for the damage it had wrought. The necessary premise, before the Court could rule on the claimants' right to compensation, was whether the bombing had been contrary to international law, thus involving the responsibility of the United States and the subsequent complicity of Japan. In the Tokyo District Court, the Japanese government asserted that there was no specific rule prohibiting the atomic bomb; besides, the launching of the two bombs had hastened Japan's surrender, thus saving many lives on both sides. It added that the protest sent on 10 August 1945 by Japan to the United States was the 'assertion as a belligerent' that the bomb was an illegal weapon; however (the Japanese government went on) 'taking an objective view, no longer in the position of a belligerent, we cannot necessarily draw the same conclusion today'.

The Court did not share this questionable view, the result of merely political considerations. It ruled that the bombing of the two towns was unlawful under international law because it infringed the two principles, one against superfluous suffering, the other against the indiscriminate use of arms. (However, the damages claimed by the plaintiffs were denied, for reasons based on Japanese domestic law.)

Did rational and viable alternatives exist?

After my remarks on how baseless Truman's arguments were and how exact were Japan's observations in its protest, the conclusions to be drawn should be clear. Though ambiguous and generic, the international legal rules on weapons do allow us to assess what happened in Hiroshima and Nagasaki. The dramatically exceptional and 'pathological' nature of those bombings leads us to conclude that, then as now, law prohibited and prohibits such inhuman acts. The arguments by which the Allies justified their actions, though very cleverly exploiting the ambiguity of the precepts, were fairly flimsy and can easily be seen for what they are: lawyers' attempts to manipulate the law and adapt it to the political and military interests of those who use force.

This conclusion, in turn, is open to two critical remarks. Some may object that it is futile to declare that the United

States violated the fundamental principles of behaviour, if such a declaration is not followed by sanctions. It is easy to rebut this argument. There are numerous cases in which the transgressors of legal rules go unpunished, in the field of international law as in that of domestic law (think, for example, of criminal law, where breaches are often not followed by the punishment of the guilty party; or of constitutional law, frequently violated by the supreme state authorities, without their being appreciably reprimanded). What is important is that the relevant legal rule should exist and that it should not be obliterated by repeated transgressions. In our case, the rule does exist, as I have tried to show. To declare that the United States did not abide by that rule is to say that it behaved in a manner contrary to the dictates of humanity and civilization embodied in the relevant legal precepts (and, therefore, solemnly accepted by the United States, as well as by other members of the international community). World public opinion must bear this in mind and see to it that other violations do not occur in future.

A second objection could be that it is easy for jurists to apportion responsibilities and guilt after politicians and the military have acted; it is far less easy for the latter to make vital decisions in the 'heat of the battle', above all when there are no other acceptable solutions which would avoid violating the law. To put it in more abstract terms: can one allow international law – which is usually a set of restraints, intended to curb and direct the actions of states – to act as a stumbling block even in exceptional circumstances, when no *alternatives* to violation exist that are in accordance with the political and strategic interests of a Great Power?

To my mind we must reject out of hand the suggestion that no *useful alternative existed that conformed with the law* in our particular case. The most significant and acceptable alternative was put forward by the Franck Committee, set up to examine the social and political implications of using the atomic bomb. On 11 June 1945 – two months before the two Japanese towns were bombed – it handed its report to President Truman, via the official channels of the War Ministry.[22] Made up of seven eminent American scientists (including Leo Szilard), the Committee suggested that, at the most, Truman should use the bomb in the desert or on an uninhabited island, simply as a demonstration (so as to force Japan to comprehend its terrifying potential and capitulate). The report added: 'after such a demonstration the weapon might perhaps be used against Japan if the sanction of the United Nations (and of public opinion at home) were obtained, perhaps after a preliminary ultimatum to Japan to surrender or at least to evacuate certain regions as an alternative to their total destruction.' Besides, to go back to a theme I dealt with earlier, the ultimatum could have contained a clause saying that the person and the dynasty of the Emperor would be preserved, in line with Stimson's suggestions which Truman, alas, rejected out of hand.

This alternative would certainly have been preferable, since the other involved the mass annihilation of human lives, after quite indescribable suffering. It would have been useful on both a political and military level because it allowed the United States to retain the 'bargaining power' (even over the other Allies) that such a horrific weapon conferred on its owner. However, this alternative had already been examined and rejected by the Interim Committee chaired by Stimson and made up of eight people (both scientists and politicians), charged with making recommendations to President Truman. After discussing the matter with the four scientists (the nuclear physicists Compton, Fermi, Lawrence and Oppenheimer) on 1 June 1945 the Committee said that either to explode the bomb on an uninhabited island or to give Japan preliminary and detailed warning, were 'impracticable'. As Stimson wrote, the two alternatives:

> were not regarded as likely to be effective in compelling a surrender of Japan, and both of them involved serious risks. Even the New Mexico test would not give final proof that any given bomb was certain to explode when dropped from an airplane. Quite apart from the generally unfamiliar nature of atomic explosives, there was the whole problem of exploding a bomb at a predetermined height in the air by a complicated mechanism which could not be tested in the static test of New Mexico. Nothing would have been more damaging to our effort to obtain surrender than a warning or a demonstration followed by a dud – and this was a real possibility. Furthermore, we had no bombs to waste.. It was vital that a sufficient effect be quickly obtained with the few we had.[23]

These arguments are harrowing. The Committee was weighing the mass destruction of innocent lives by the use of a weapon with terrible effects, both military and political, against the possible loss of prestige by a Great Power if it made a mess of things after announcing the use of a new, devastating weapon. To the US government the latter outweighed the former! What can we say, then, of the argument that the United States had so few bombs at its disposal, that a merely demonstrative explosion would be a 'waste'! Besides, as Leo Szilard (who saw it all from the 'inside' because he had worked on the bomb from the beginning) remarked, it would have taken very little time to get the number of bombs up to ten.[24] Thus, this second argument was basically without foundation. I should add that, in any case, the arguments of the Interim Committee were less 'utilitarian' than those advanced by James Byrnes (at the time, the President's representative on the Committee) against Leo Szilard who pleaded that the bomb should not be used. Byrnes remarked that the US government had spent two billion dollars on developing the bomb and that Congress would enquire how that money had been invested. He added that it would be difficult in future to get Congress to foot the bill for research on atomic energy if no tangible proof were offered of the results so far obtained.[25]

But let us return to the main point in the Franck report. The scientists not only suggested that President Truman should follow a plausible and relatively rational alternative, they also indicated quite clearly why to use the bomb could be very dangerous *for the future*. The report backed up its theory with two main points. In the 'optimistic' event that an international agreement banning the use of the atomic bomb were soon reached, it would be difficult to persuade the world that the United States seriously intended to respect a ban on the atomic bomb after it had already used one, to devastating and inhuman effect: lack of confidence in, or suspicion of, the United States after such a bombing would be a formidable obstacle to any ban on these weapons. On the other hand, by using the bomb to demonstrate its potential in a desert area, the United States could say to the world, in Franck's words: 'You see what sort of a weapon we had but did not use. We are ready to renounce its use in the future if other nations join us in this renunciation and agree to the establishment of an efficient international control.'

In the 'pessimistic' event of there being little chance of securing an international agreement, even the 'demonstration' would seem ill advised, because after the United States had announced its intention of using the atomic bomb, an atomic race would start, with very dangerous consequences for the whole of humanity, especially the United States (a country whose population and industries are concentrated in a relatively limited number of metropolitan areas; in case of atomic war it would, therefore, be at a disadvantage compared to countries with populations and industries spread out over a vast area). Let me add that this point was also argued with force in the 'petition' to President Truman, written on 17 July 1945 by Leo Szilard and signed by 68 American scientists; however, because of a series of hitches, the petition never reached the President's desk.[26]

Two months before the atomic bombing of Japan and six days before the experiment in the Alamogordo desert, the seven American scientists had outlined in detail the grave peril that the use of that lethal weapon implied for the future of mankind. A month later, a large number of their colleagues expressed the same fear. None of these scientists had followed *the reasoning proper to international law*, or had examined *the legal or moral lawfulness of using the atomic bomb*; they had viewed the use of that weapon from a wider standpoint, one that saw beyond the annihilation of thousands of Japanese lives. By so doing they showed they had a greater sense of history and greater foresight about the future than either Truman or Churchill. Churchill considered only the political and military domination of Japan, and relations of power and hegemony among the Great Powers (especially between East and West). By contrast, the seven scientists (as well as those who signed Leo Szilard's petition to Truman) had a complete understanding of what was at stake: not merely the lives of thousands of Japanese, nor the distribution of spheres of influence, but the whole future of mankind. In this sense, the decision to use the bomb was undoubtedly a turning point in the history of man. It conjured up a nightmare which still haunts us all today.

Some final remarks

Readers of Freud may remember those pages of his *Civilization and its Discontents* (1930) in which, after listing the various 'tools' created by man to enhance the power of his limbs and

senses (from telescopes to cameras, records, ships and
aeroplanes), he remarks that man is now equipped with so
many accessory instruments, so many artificial limbs, that he
himself has become a sort of 'artificial' god (*eine Art Prothesen-
gott*). By so doing, Freud goes on, he has achieved almost all
the dreams described in myths and almost resembles those gods
he had invented and about whom he had told stories so many
years ago, endowing them with omniscience and omnipo-
tence.[27] Today, man himself has become almost omniscient and
omnipotent.

In the 1940s this 'artificial god' invented a 'tool' that gave him
the power of maximum destruction, far beyond the mere
strength of limbs with which he had been endowed in the
beginning. By using that 'tool' he violated the fundamental
commandments on civilized intercourse that he himself had
ordained. The problem with which we are confronted today is
agonizing: can the humanity sanctioned by those 'commandments' override the 'desire for dominion' over nature and men
that led to the creation of the loathsome 'tool'? To the solution
of this problem each one of us, however small-voiced and
weak, can endeavour to make a modest contribution.

2

Why States Use Force with Impunity

The 'Black Holes' of International Law

What the 'man in the street' wants to know

Almost every day we read of cases, some serious some less so, in which states have resorted to armed attack: wars, punitive expeditions into foreign territory against terrorist bases, aeroplanes intercepted, nuclear plants bombed, hazardous operations to save nationals held hostage abroad by bands of terrorists or state authorities. In the end the 'man in the street' has formed his own 'theory' on the subject: the use of force dominates the international community and every state is free to use violence with impunity. This is Hobbes's 'state of nature', in which neither police nor firemen, still less judges, operate but only collective bodies with no effective power. The latter are the UN Security Council and the General Assembly, which are convened promptly during and after every crisis to discuss and deliberate, but whose pronouncements change nothing. Law does not exist; only the number of 'bombs' a state possesses counts.

Let us take a look at this pocket philosophy and see whether there is any justification for the sceptical view that interstate violence is inevitable because there is no legal harness by which to restrain it.[1]

From the traditional system to the UN Charter

For centuries war was sanctioned by law in the international community as a way of asserting, if somewhat brutally, a state's legal rights and for pursuing national interests. Thus war was used to annex the territory of a neighbouring state; to acquire colonies; to force a change of government on another state; to protect the economic interests of nationals abroad. Naturally if one reads one's way through the 'classics' of international law, those eminent jurists of the eighteenth and nineteenth centuries (Vattel, de Martens, Bluntschli, Heffter or Wheaton), little can be found that reflects the scale of contemporary violence in the international community, that is the full support lent by law to the use of force. They tend, rather, to underscore the rules and institutions that 'mediate' between states; they speak of the peaceful relations that exist between sovereign bodies; and, when they mention war, it is to explain that it also is subject to given rules. Everything therefore proceeds according to the harmonious dictates of legal precepts. The modern reader is tempted to dismiss all this as mere 'ideological' theorizing; however, this would be an over-simplification because it ignores one important point: these same jurists played an essential role in the formation of European and US diplomats and politicians. Their ideological 'manipulation' of reality led mainly to positive results, because they instilled in the minds of statesmen and international actors the idea that there were rules and these had to be obeyed, at least in everyday transactions and in matters of no vital importance (whenever the supreme interests of states were involved, the requirements of sovereignty were, obviously, reasserted).

However, a realistic picture of international relations is to be found in the pages of some of the greatest political thinkers: Hobbes, Montesquieu, Kant and Rousseau. They saw quite clearly how arbitrary was the power that existed in interstate relations and how it received the full support of law. Though not in strictly juridical terms, they perceived and described the concept of 'self-help' – a concept that jurists were only to elaborate with difficulty at the turn of the last century. This would allow every state to choose for itself the nature and extent of its own interests, to enquire for itself whether another subject has trampled those interests underfoot and, then, to decide for itself if and how to impose sanctions for these violations. In other words, in the traditional international community the situation resembled that of certain American 'westerns', in which a sheriff either does not exist or has no power, the judge lives far away, and every member of the village must protect his own rights and interests with his fists and his gun.

To return to our own time, the situation today looks different – at least on a formal level and, to a certain extent, on an institutional level. When, in 1945 in San Francisco, the UN Charter was approved, a radical turning point was marked – at least this is what the 'founding fathers' had hoped. Many statesmen had been profoundly shocked by the Second World War and they ardently desired to set up an institution capable of preventing the repetition of such large-scale tragedy. The Charter system was based on three fundamental 'pillars'. First, not armed force alone, but even its threat, were banned forever (article 2, paragraph 4 of the Charter). Second, a collective body, the UN Security Council, was empowered to act as policeman: should a violation of peace and international security occur, or even the mere threat to peace, it could send its armed forces (placed at its disposal at an earlier date by the various member states) to the trouble spot. Third, in exceptional circumstances, a state could defend itself as long as it was the victim of armed attack, and until such time as the Security Council itself intervened; in other words, 'self-defence' was allowed (article 51). It corresponded, more or less, to the form foreseen in all state law (if someone is about to kill me, I have the right to prevent my aggressor from doing so either by killing him or by neutralizing him; that is if I have not had time to call in the police). In addition, under the UN Charter this self-defence could be 'individual' (I have been attacked and am defending myself on my own) or 'collective' (I rush in to help another who has been attacked and had already requested my help in anticipation of future attack, or had asked for it as soon as the attack began).

These were the three main bastions of the Charter. However, they were supported by a fourth postulate, that was never given explicit expression, but was very much alive in the minds of the statesmen and diplomats gathered together in San Francisco: apart from self-defence, the use of force on the territory of another state could be justified with its *consent*. In other words, in 1945 it was taken for granted that a state member could ask another state to use force on its territory, for example in civil war. The principle of consent (*volenti non fit injuria*) was a natural and essential one in the traditional international community (in which a state could consent to anything, even to its own dismemberment or extinction) and in 1945 it was not thought necessary to sanction it explicitly. Perhaps the drafters did not realize that the Charter proclaimed other principles, almost always explicitly, that could conflict with the principle of consent. Take, for example, the principle of the self-determination of peoples, of non-interference in domestic affairs, or of respect for human rights; in cases of conflict, which was to prevail? (For instance, one state asks another to send in its army to participate in the massacre of those of its citizens that belong to a certain ethnic group, or to suffocate by violent means the will of the majority of its population to choose a democratic regime). In 1945, this problem was left open.

End of a magnificent illusion: the security system set up in 1945 breaks down

The mechanism set up in San Francisco could have worked if the cold war had not broken out at once and the world had not split into two blocks. It is easy to imagine the effects of this rift on the 'system of collective security'. The 'armed forces' of the United Nations were never created; the West, which had the majority in the General Assembly, tried to deflect to the General Assembly the powers that had been attributed to the Security Council (blocked by the Soviet veto); the tension grew and the whole collective mechanism broke down. The result was twofold though it was not simultaneous, deriving in either case from the failure of the centralized system set up in 1945. First, the small and middle-sized states opted for the 'protection' of one of the two Great Powers to create a sort of buffer against attacks from the other camp. This led to the creation of NATO (1949) and of the Warsaw Pact (1955). The result was a total failure of the 1945 attempt to bypass the traditional system of politico-military alliances and a return to the system of antagonistic alliances. Deprived of a real 'police force', a group of 'vigilantes' was set up, a mere surrogate for the armed forces foreseen in the Charter. Thus the 'blue berets' were created but, in moments of international crisis, they could not use force against the belligerents and had to stand in the middle to keep them from flying at each other's throats; all this with the mere wave of a baton. The new system (called 'peace-keeping operations') has worked moderately well on several occasions (Suez, 1956–67; Congo, 1960–1; Cyprus, from 1964 on; the Middle East, from 1973 on). However, intrinsic limitations to such 'policing' operations were soon revealed and the United Nations gradually abandoned the use of 'blue berets'.

Little by little, states were left on their own, or segregated in groups of allies, to face crisis and assert their rights. Bit by bit, the old system of self-help was reinstated: every nation on its own had to see that justice was done. Well, not quite. It was now impossible to return to pre-Charter days for political, diplomatic and psychological reasons; no state now believed it was advisable to allow the UN system, however leaky, to sink without trace. Indeed, the system was a useful point of reference and was of considerable political and institutional value. The majority of principles and rules of behaviour sanctioned by the Charter, as well as the institutional mechanism set up in 1945, despite their manifold defects, still formed a *bulwark against total anarchy* as long as they were kept alive. But how could this need for peace and order be reconciled with the necessity of using violence whenever national interests were at stake? Besides, the latter was not always the result of the desire for supremacy of the Great Powers. In a community where the use of force is prohibited in rigorous terms (article 2, paragraph 4 of the UN Charter), but with no effective system of collective sanctions of an institutional nature to be applied in cases of transgression, a state that is the victim of violations faces a dramatic dilemma: either it submits passively to violence, or it reacts and by so doing probably violates the rules of the community.

The solution to this dilemma was not to abolish the Charter rules, nor to insist on a passive acceptance of violations perpetrated by others, but to reach a *compromise*; when all is said and done, this has at least the virtue of keeping alive, to a large extent, what was still vital in the San Francisco system and, at the same time, of *channelling state violence*. The solution consisted in a rereading and amplification of the only explicit permissive rule contained in the Charter (article 51) which, as I have already said, sanctioned self-defence. At an *interpretative level*, states had gradually widened the meshes of that authorization, to increase its permissiveness, and extended its scope to areas that were unthought of in 1945. At the same time, the role played by the other 'loophole' allowed, implicitly, by the Charter was increased; that is, the consent of a state on whose territory another state intends to use force.

These two routes have led to our present-day solution. I shall now attempt to pinpoint the concrete ways by which some states (especially the Great Powers and the middle-sized ones which they support) have forced the meaning of the two 'safety valves' inserted in the Charter. Then, I shall try to answer a question that comes immediately to mind: what has been done to oppose or attenuate the 'forcing' I have just mentioned? To put it differently, how did the other states and the UN bodies react? Did they approve, or did they raise objections? In more general terms, when the traditional rules are 'manipulated' or 'perverted', are there any mechanisms by which condemnation can be expressed or the effect of these manipulations limited?

How states have developed the permissive rules of the Charter ever since the cold war began

One of the first attempts to widen the meshes of the network of rules created in 1945 was to argue that article 51 authorizes not only self-defence against an aggression in full swing, but also *preventive* self-defence, whenever an attack is expected. It is pointed out that in the international community things work differently than in a state community. If I happen to learn that a man intends to break into my house and rob me, I telephone the police and ask them to arrest the thief. In the international community, if one knows an attack is imminent there is no kind saint ready to listen to one's prayers for help. The best defence is almost always to attack at once and break up the enemy forces before they have time to move. This necessity, it is pointed out, is all the more compelling in a nuclear age, an age of missiles and jet planes. Should I discover that a neighbouring state is getting ready to launch an offensive with sophisticated, lightning weapons, why wait until the missiles and jets cross over into my airspace before reacting? Naturally, the arguments for military necessity are given the full support of legal reasoning (briefly, it is emphasized that article 51, in allowing an *'inherent* right to self-defence', wished to preserve the pre-existing law, which undoubtedly – so they say – allowed for preventive self-defence as well). These arguments, as well as the right to resort to preventive self-defence, were invoked by Israel in 1967 (against Egypt), in 1975 (against Lebanon) and in 1981 (after the attack on the nuclear plant near Baghdad) and by Iraq in 1980 to justify its attack on Iran.

Another way of broadening the scope of the 'authorizations' in the Charter is to assert that self-defence allows a state to react against enemy attack not only when this has been launched on its territory or against its ships, but also when the 'victims' of the attack are its *nationals* abroad. Thus, every time state authorities, terrorists or armed bands threaten the lives and property of foreigners, the state whose nationals the latter are can intervene with its army to protect them. This justification has been invoked more than once, usually by Western states to legitimize the use of force in Third World countries. The Belgians did so for the Congo in 1960 and 1964; the Israelis for Entebbe (Uganda) in 1976; the United States justified the use of force in the Dominican Republic in 1965, their intervention to save the crew of the *Mayaguez* in 1975, their botched attempt to rescue the US hostages held in Tehran in 1980 and the sending of troops into Grenada in 1983, all with the same argument.

Yet another way of broadening the scope for the use of force is to assert that the armed attack, mentioned in article 51 to authorize self-defence, can take the form not only of direct aggression, but also – and ever more frequently – of an *indirect armed aggression*. This can be twofold: either 'volunteers' or mercenaries are sent together with weapons and munitions etc. to rebels fighting in another country against the legitimate government; or 'terrorist' or rebel groups receive hospitality and training facilities, new weapons and so on, before launching an attack on another country. In either case, it is said, the state that is attacked by the 'volunteers', or by the rebels or terrorists that use 'sanctuaries' in another state, must try to put down the potential violence by attacking it at its source; it must hit at the heart of the state that sends in 'volunteers' or conveys arms to them, or gives 'sanctuary' to terrorists and rebels. These arguments have been used by numerous states. The second form of indirect aggression provoked Israel, more than once, to attack the Palestinian bases in Lebanon (1970–83) and Tunisia (1985); it was behind Rhodesia's attack on Zambia (1978–9) and South Africa's military operations (between 1976 and 1985) in Zambia, Lesotho, Angola and Swaziland. The first kind of indirect armed aggression has provoked the reaction of both Western states and the Soviet Union: among other instances were the US intervention in Lebanon (1958), that of Great Britain in Jordan (1958), and that of the USSR in Czechoslovakia (1968) and Afghanistan (1979).

Another attempt to inject into the Charter values that it either did not contain, or allowed only in very cautious terms, was made by Third World countries. They have repeatedly asserted that colonialism is a form of 'permanent aggression' that a colonial power wages against a foreign people. That people not only have the right to fight against the aggressor, but third states have the right to intervene and help it achieve freedom, with force if necessary, thereby exercising a right to 'collective self-defence'. These arguments were advanced by India in 1961, when it sent its troops into the tiny Portuguese colony of Goa (an enclave in Indian territory) to put an end to Portuguese 'aggression' that, as the Indian delegate said to the Security Council, had lasted for centuries. On that occasion the Soviet veto saved India from censure. However, the USSR did not feel it could support Argentina in 1982 when the latter occupied the Falkland/Malvinas islands: the Security Council condemned the Argentine military attack despite the latter's argument, among other points, that British colonialism in the area was a form of 'permanent aggression'.

A further justification for the use of violence was discovered in the principle that a state can legitimately authorize another to use force on its territory: in other words, the principle of *consent*. It is usually invoked when a territorial state, torn asunder by rebellion, and a second state (called on to intervene) both assert that only military aid from abroad can help the territorial state put an end to the rebellion. The most famous cases in which the argument was used were Hungary (1956), when the USSR sent in its battalions to suppress the revolt, Czechoslovakia (1968) and Afghanistan (1979). The United States also invoked the principle as one of the reasons for its intervention in Lebanon (1958) and Grenada (1983). In almost all these cases it was by no means certain that the *legitimate* government had really requested the intervention of the Great Power. (From this point of view, the Soviet intervention in Czechoslovakia and Afghanistan and the American one in Grenada are particularly significant.)

Let me recall now a few instances in which the use of force was not justified by invoking the two 'traditional' and most common 'legal titles' (self-defence and the consent of the state on whose territory the acts of violence are perpetrated), but by referring to other reasons.

Some states (Israel frequently and South Africa on occasion) say that *armed reprisals* are justified, at least in exceptional circumstances (for example, when the lack of any 'violent' reaction to repeated attacks on a State's territory resulting in serious loss of life and damage to the property of its citizens, would appear to authorize these violations or make the state under attack seem indifferent to their recurrence in the future). In such a case, recourse to measures of coercion normally forbidden by the UN Charter is justified, they say, because the Charter system of collective security is paralysed and, thus, single states are justified in 'recovering' certain rights theoretically 'suppressed' in 1945; among these, the right to react with force against terrorist acts that are tolerated by foreign states.

In other cases some states have tried to justify the use of force by saying that they had to react against the grave violations of human rights committed by the state in whose territory force had been used. The justification of a 'humanitarian intervention' was invoked, more or less explicitly, by India when it sent its troops into Eastern Pakistan (now Bangladesh) in 1971. The idea of 'humanitarian intervention' was also put forward for Tanzania, after its invasion of Uganda in 1979.

Finally, one expedient – used mainly by the United States – to put a legal cloak on the use of force, is to invoke the rules of regional organizations. According to the United States, when it is certain or highly probable that the Security Council will be blocked by the veto of one of its permanent members, a state can legitimately obtain the *collective* consent or authorization to use force from a regional organization. On this basis the United States initiated the famous 'quarantine' on Cuba, during the missile crisis (1962), and sent its troops into the Dominican Republic (1965) and Grenada (1983).

Let me conclude this rapid survey by underscoring one point

that should already have become apparent: whenever states decide to use force, they prefer to invoke *more than one justification*, because they then feel safer from diplomatic and political objections. Thus, even if one justification is criticized or disputed, the others help to put a legal 'mask' on the use of force.

What is it that allows states to 'manipulate' the Charter principles?

How could the Great Powers, and other states directly or indirectly supported by them, use force so often and find so many formal justifications in article 51, in the principle of consent and in other Charter rules? In other words, how can states suggest interpretations of international rules as suits them best, bending the law to their own personal interests? The answer is quite simple: in the international community there are no judges to 'declare the law' with binding effect on all subjects. To a large extent, the system is one of self-interpretation. Naturally, the system becomes enormously important when it deals with legal rules that regulate the most crucial and delicate aspects of international relations, in other words those that touch the raw flesh of things and directly affect the vital interests of states, whether political, economic or military. As I have already had occasion to observe, these are areas where states, both great and middle-sized, deliberately leave law in a condition of inexactitude and uncertainty, if not ambiguity, making it easier for them to protect their own interests. The point is that the Charter, especially article 51 and the principle of consent, is full of 'black holes', or shadowy areas in which, since there are no judges, every state is free to lend the rule the interpretation it thinks fit.

How can the arbitrary interpretations of states be limited? The gradual crystallization of interpretative tendencies that legitimize the use of force

Let me ask one more question here: is there any common way by which states could agree once and for all on the most correct interpretation, or at least one that could become binding, of the Charter principles? The answer is easy: the only way to achieve this would be to *create rules* that describe and circumscribe the concept of self-defence and the limits within which consent is applicable. In the international community these rules can be created in one of two ways: either by *agreement* between all the members of the United Nations; or by the gradual emergence of a tacit agreement among states, in other words the development of a *custom*. Predictably, states – expecially poor and defenceless states – have trodden both paths, trying to draw the Great Powers in their wake, with little success. In 1970 the General Assembly approved by *consensus* (in effect, by unanimity) a famous 'Declaration on Friendly Relations', which tried to make more accurate and update the Charter rules on the use of force. This declaration was followed in 1974 by the equally famous 'Definition of Aggression', also passed by the General Assembly by consensus. However, neither of the two declarations introduced many new ideas and these only in marginal areas. Besides, they were not given binding force, that is they were never considered international agreements properly. In practice the basic problems remained unsolved, mainly because the great and middle-sized states were not prepared to discuss anew the central points of the existing system and risk upsetting the delicate balance that had been created, to their own advantage, in the application of the Charter rules.

Let us now take a look at their application in practice to see whether there is any sign of agreement, at least on some points, on what can and what cannot be done. Not much has been accomplished; though the situation is not altogether disappointing. Briefly, some measure of agreement has been reached, not on creating new rules, but on the interpretation of existing rules, especially article 51 of the Charter. Let me just mention the points on which some form of agreement has been reached.

The first is the problem of *preventive* self-defence: it can be said that it is accepted now only in exceptional circumstances, when a state has solid and reliable proof that an armed aggression is imminent and of such magnitude as to endanger the very survival of the nation. This view is supported by the fact that when, in 1967, Israel forestalled Egypt's attack, neither the Security Council nor the General Assembly condemned its actions; whereas there was open condemnation in 1981 of Israel's attack on the nuclear plant in Iraq (in this particular case, it was clear from numerous pieces of evidence that Iraq had not been preparing for an armed attack).

Second, it would appear that the use of force to protect one's *nationals abroad* is accepted only when their lives are being immediately and indisputably threatened by the territorial state or by terrorists (against whom the territorial government either cannot or will not act) and that all possible routes to a peaceful solution have been tried without success.

Third, in cases of *indirect armed aggression* the practice is to prohibit the use of force against 'rebels' or 'terrorists' hosted in foreign 'sanctuaries'. This is the meaning to be construed from the pronouncements of the various bodies of the United Nations after Israel's attacks on Lebanon (1970–83) and Tunisia (1985); those of South Africa on Zambia (1976 and 1980), Lesotho (1982), Angola (1976, 1978, 1980, 1984) and Swaziland (1985); and Southern Rhodesia's attacks on Botswana (1977) and Zambia (1978 and 1979). In regard to the practice of indirect armed aggression, which consists in sending 'volunteers', UN practice and, above all, its pronouncements on the Soviet intervention in Czechoslovakia (1968) and Afghanistan (1979) show that force can be used only when there is certain and irrefutable proof that a third state is about to send in its armed forces, even under the guise of 'volunteers' or mercenaries; whereas, proof of the sending of arms and munitions or the giving of logistic help of any kind to the rebels, is not enough. This view has recently received the support of the International Court of Justice in the *Nicaragua* v. *U.S.* case. Where *consent* is the legitimizing factor in an armed intervention, the tendency is to require that it be given, without any shadow of doubt, by the lawful government. Besides, whether it had been requested or authorized, the intervention must not suppress the right to self-determination of the people dwelling in the territory where the intervention is taking place; nor can it be in the form of undue interference in domestic affairs; and, finally, it cannot violate human rights, or eventually entail such a violation.

Finally, it seems that the cloak provided by *regional organizations* has not received unanimous consent because, so far, it has been used mainly by the United States to justify military actions on the American continent. Possibly, especially in situations similar to the missile crisis in Cuba (1962), the collective authorization of a regional organization might be an acceptable justification, at least in specific circumstances (which did not exist in the Cuban crisis, so that the United States acted unlawfully then).

How other possible forms of violence have been made unlawful

This quick glance at how states tend to legitimize certain forms of violence would be incomplete if I did not give an idea of the various routes that the majority of the members of the United Nations have closed to other possible uses of force (suggested by a few nations). Perhaps the most important aspect of the way international affairs have evolved after 1945 has been precisely to have stated clearly that some categories of violence can have no political or legal justification and are, therefore, destined to arouse lively and widespread disapproval in the 'society of nations'. I shall just mention three of the 'culs-de-sac' that I feel are particularly significant.

The first is the possible recourse to armed force to *react against the wrong of another that fell short of force*. As I mentioned earlier, quite a few states and numerous jurists have supported the legitimacy of armed reprisals against nations that disobey international rules without, however, using force (for example, they pay no heed to the decision of the International Court of Justice, or violate an important commercial treaty or a fundamental customary rule on the treatment of foreigners). In such cases, say these states and jurists, if the victim that has suffered the unlawful act is powerless to impose 'effective' sanctions then any transgression of international law would become permissible: the UN Charter would end by 'rewarding' those responsible and by 'punishing' the victims. This form of reasoning has been successfully refuted by it being pointed out that the Charter (in article 51) clearly allows the use of force only against unlawful acts that are so serious as to become military aggressions; if every state, as the victim of a wrong, could retaliate by means of armed reprisals (and not just peaceful reprisals, such as the similar violation of a treaty, economic sanctions, etc.), the foundations would be laid for dangerous escalations of violence – all more so when the act is determined to have been unlawful by the 'victim' alone, thus opening the way to obvious abuses. Here, again, this view has been upheld by the International Court of Justice in its recent decision, referred to above (*Nicaragua* v. *U.S.*).

Another instance of use of force that has finally been excluded refers to *national wars of liberation*. As I have already said, towards the end of the 1950s various socialist and numerous Third World countries asserted that national liberation movements – which, in their opinion, qualified as international subjects – had a right to fight against colonial powers or 'oppressor' states, thanks to the rule on self-defence. Consequently, by virtue of article 51 of the Charter, every state that felt political sympathy for or was friendly towards a national liberation movement could use force to help the movement and so exercise its right to 'collective self-defence'. The military and political consequences of this are obvious: the international legitimation of violence would lead to the proliferation of international conflict and also to an escalation of violence. Indeed, while many states would fly to the side of the national liberation movements (especially socialist and developing nations), other governments would be induced to help the colonial or 'oppressor' state, and the breeding-grounds for violence would multiply. Fortunately, this theory was finally exploded and a more moderate and realistic one has taken its place. Today third states can help national liberation movements by sending arms and munitions, by giving logistic and medical help, but they cannot send in their own armed forces. If they do so, they are no longer exercising a right, but are committing an offence; or rather, they are violating the ban on the use of force contained in article 2, paragraph 4.

The international community also rejected the idea of *humanitarian intervention*. This can be deduced from the negative reactions of other states to the two cases I mentioned earlier (India's intervention in Eastern Pakistan in 1971, and Tanzania's in Uganda in 1979), and also to Vietnam's invasion of Cambodia in 1978, when several states declared in the United Nations that, despite the atrocities committed by the Khmer Rouge, Vietnam had no right to invade its neighbour.

Limits to these interpretative tendencies: the 'black holes' have not been removed

As we can see, in practice there has been considerable agreement among states, leading to the crystallization of certain acceptable 'interpretative guidelines' and the rejection of others. This must not fill us with unrealistic hope for the future. I have merely pointed to certain tendencies that, in my opinion, have emerged over the past few years and that seem to be confirmed by the attitudes of states and of the supreme UN bodies. Even though it is true that every state is held in check by the interpretative rules that have emerged, it is also true that those rules are not in the form of rigorous and well-defined criteria. For the time being, these rules should be considered the *political and diplomatic road signs* of the international community. Their main purpose is to remind states that if they respect these standards they will receive the approval of the whole community; should they fail to respect them, they will provoke the political and moral condemnation of other states. Nevertheless, the 'black holes' are still there and it is hard to imagine that they will be rapidly eliminated: international law is still uncertain and full of loopholes and, above all, it receives no support from effective institutional guarantees. As I have said more than once, the use of force is a subject that touches on the vital interests of states, especially as far as the Great Powers are concerned. It is therefore unlikely that it will ever be subject to rigorous and operative legal discipline.

What, then, is the value of the Charter principles, or of these interpretative tendencies? States consider these rules of behaviour useful above all from a political and diplomatic point of view. Individuals, private groups and public opinion find them useful as *guidelines* for judging the actions of states. If they did not exist, one would hardly know how to assess the individual actions of nations. They help us determine whether a given state has conformed to the standards of behaviour of the international community. Besides, except in special circumstances, our own opinion will correspond to the approval or condemnation expressed by the supreme political bodies of the international community: the Security Council and the General Assembly. Thus, the 'man in the street', public opinion (and the media that ought to keep it informed) as well as the collegiate bodies of the international community all have a 'decalogue' by which to judge the actions of states. True, there are no corresponding *legal sanctions*: all we can offer are political and moral sanctions. The absence of judges and policemen is an evil to which we must resign ourselves without complaining too loudly, secure in the knowledge that law at least offers the necessary parameters for forming a moral and political opinion.

3

Is the First Use of Nuclear Weapons Prohibited?

An overture

As we all know, from the late 1950s on, a strategy of deterrence has ensured that there have been no nuclear wars: both of the two great powers are well aware that, should one launch a nuclear attack on the other, the latter will retaliate by launching a massive 'reprisal' against the metropolitan areas of the attacker. It has rightly been said that whereas in the past the sons of kings were given as hostages to ensure respect for a peace treaty, today the sons of the cities – that is all of us who live in towns, large or small – are held hostage by each great power to guarantee that a nuclear war is never launched.

Although this balance of terror is meant essentially to avoid the first use of nuclear weapons, the first strike has not been banished from military strategy and therefore is still included among the hypotheses of what might happen. First, the United States has stated more than once that, considering the Warsaw Pact's definite superiority in conventional weapons both in Europe and other areas, the nuclear powers of the North Atlantic pact cannot rule out the possibility of using nuclear weapons first, in reaction to a massive use of conventional arms by the USSR against Western Europe or South Korea.[1] Second, some American experts have suggested that, given present conditions, it would be to the Soviet Union's 'advantage' to launch a nuclear attack on the West, despite the consequent destruction of numerous metropolitan areas in the USSR.[2] Similarly, if and when the SDI (Strategic Defence Initiative, commonly known as 'Star Wars') is set up, then possibly the USSR might feel obliged to launch a nuclear attack on the United States to prevent the strategy of deterrence from becoming obsolete as a result of SDI. Third, some highly respected experts suspect that one of the minor nuclear powers might feel it is to its advantage to solve a serious case of political conflict by using nuclear arms.[3]

As we can see, present-day strategic 'theory' has suggested the possibility of both a 'first use' and a 'second use' of nuclear weapons in the guise of a massive reprisal. Now, what has international law to say about these two possibilities? Does it feel impotent to regulate issues that are so fatally decisive for mankind; or does it interpose its authority and speak out loudly on the subject? If the latter is the case, what does international law do? Does it *authorize* the use of nuclear arms in the knowledge that, on their own, legal precepts can do little to restrain that use? Or, does it *condemn* these arms by banning them in categorical terms? Or, alternatively, does it *timidly counsel* states to avoid unleashing such destructive forces?

Is it worth asking such questions?

If one poses questions such as these, one is immediately faced with two snares that can entangle the questioner even before one begins to explore this area of terrible uncertainty. The first is the scepticism of those who firmly believe that states pay no heed to moral tenets and legal rules when their vital interests are at stake. How futile, they say, to ask whether there are rules of conduct that ought to curb the actions of states since, even if they do exist, those states would certainly take no notice of them.

The second snare is equally difficult to avoid. It is extremely difficult to discern whether these parameters exist at all and, if they do, how widespread is their effect. Thus, it is hardly surprising when a distinguished jurist who had written that a general rule banning the use of nuclear weapons does exist, changed his mind (in the second edition of his book) and concluded that the rule had never crystallized.[4]

The issue is undoubtedly a thorny one. But surely that is no reason not to examine it. We shall have to advance over the terrain with circumspection, weigh the proof over and over again and never believe that our assessments are final. Above all, we shall have to eschew the trap of a *rigid alternative*. Not a few jurists, in just such a quest, have fallen into that trap: some have stated categorically that law prohibits the use of nuclear arms, while others have declared with equal self-assurance that law undoubtedly leaves states free to act as they please.

The first objection, that it is useless to ask such questions, is the most serious. It should, therefore, be faced head on. I feel it is entirely wrong. In the Introduction I have already said that, after taking a careful look at international affairs, it is remarkable how often states do not neglect legal imperatives, when these are clearly stated. In areas of vital military importance, the Great Powers have adopted various strategies to prevent the emergence of rules of conduct that would limit their actions. Consequently, our dilemma is not simply whether or not a ban on the use of nuclear weapons exists. It is far more complex and goes as follows: if such a ban exists, is it free of ambiguity, or does it leave international subjects plenty of room to sail round it? How effective is it? Can it really curb the actions of states, or is it a device of rhetorical and political value only? If one decides that the ban has never crystallized, then what political and military forces prevented its formation and is there any hope that it may crystallize in the future?

If these are the questions to which we must find an answer, it is worth doing so, if only because it will help us gain a better understanding of the motives that inspire the Great Powers in a crucial area.

Some preliminary distinctions

The question I posed in the title to this essay merely refers to the first use of nuclear weapons, because the second strike is universally acknowledged as lawful. It would be patently absurd and also contrary to the law to assert that a state cannot use nuclear weapons to retaliate against the nuclear attack launched by another state. In such a case, and even if it were launched only against the aggressor's civilian population, to employ nuclear arms would obviously be legitimate, despite the horrifying consequences. Of course, if the belligerent follows a strategy of 'controlled escalation' and uses tactical nuclear weapons, or limits his attack to precise military objectives, the other side is expected to respond accordingly and in proportion and, above all, to avoid hitting the enemy's civilian population.

By 'first use' I mean that a belligerent resorts to a nuclear weapon before another state has used that *same weapon*, or before it has made *extensive use of prohibited weapons of mass destruction* (such as chemical or bacteriological arms). Indeed, should these weapons ever be used on a large scale, the other side might be forced to 'respond' with nuclear weapons against such a macroscopic instance of violation of the law of war. Naturally, the response must be 'restrained' that is 'proportionate' to the attack; besides, a nuclear weapon should be used only as a *last resort*, because it is so dangerous and would transform a conventional war into a nuclear war for both sides.

The legal frames of reference

From a legal point of view the first use of nuclear weapons falls within the purview of *two separate groups of international rules:* those on *force* in general (contained in the UN Charter) and the more specific rules on the use of *weapons* (or, as we shall see, principles embodied in the law of war). These two 'clusters' of precepts were created by states to control their own actions by means of a stringent and rigorous network of laws. In theory, at least, the two groups of rules should buttress one another and (together) block any undue recourse to armed violence.

The first body of rules (described in the preceding essay) does allow a state to justify the use of nuclear weapons as a form of self-defence. If nuclear weapons are used to counteract a massive attack by an enemy (using conventional weapons, whether legal or illegal), then a state can invoke the right to 'subsequent' self-defence (article 51 of the Charter). If, on the other hand, a state is the first to launch a nuclear attack, intending to destroy the enemy before he has time to move, it can invoke the right to pre-emptive self-defence (which, according to many, is provided for in the same article 51). It is precisely the ambiguity of this Charter rule and the contradictory interpretations given it by various nations that enable states to claim as *legitimate* the use of nuclear arms. As I remarked in an earlier essay, legitimate preventive self-defence is admissible only in *exceptional* circumstances: when certain and irrefutable proof exists that a massive armed attack – such as to endanger a state's very survival – is about to be launched and there is no alternative to a pre-emptive nuclear strike. One has only to list these conditions to show how, in case of nuclear war, one of the Great Powers could unblushingly claim they existed and proceed to attack its antagonist. Thus, in prohibiting *recourse to force*, international law is not able to guard effectively against the first use of a nuclear weapon.

Let us now see whether international law is equally feeble in applying the relative bans on the *specific use of a nuclear weapon*.

The two traditional bans

The first use of nuclear weapons is covered by the ban contained in the two traditional general principles on the use of any military device. These ban weapons that cause unnecessary suffering, as well as those that strike civilians and soldiers indiscriminately.

Unhappily, we know enough about the atomic bomb to say that its effects are so devastating as to violate both these principles. However, it has been claimed that the latest and most sophisticated nuclear weapons can be 'clean' or 'smart', in other words they are able to strike military targets exclusively. Naturally, it is hard to know if this is in fact true and let us hope that, for lack of concrete proof, our doubts will linger long. In 1983 the World Health Organization asked a group of eminent scientists from various parts of the world (including the United States and the USSR) to make a detailed report on the effects of nuclear arms. The report concluded that if nuclear weapons were used, there could be three possible scenarios. First, a bomb of one megaton is dropped on a large city such as London; in this case there would be about a million and a half dead and the same number wounded. Second, if the nuclear war is 'limited' to the use of smaller tactical nuclear weapons (to a total of twenty megatons) against military objectives in an area with a fairly high population density, there would be about nine million dead and seriously wounded people, of which over eight million would be civilians. Third, in a total nuclear war, using about half the present potential stock (about 10,000 megatons), there would be over a billion dead and as many wounded.[5]

In any of the three hypothetical situations a large number of civilians would die. Thus, any recourse to nuclear arms would be contrary to the ban on indiscriminate weapons.

However, let us suppose that it is possible to use a 'clean' nuclear weapon in such a way as to hit only military objectives. Then, since those who are not killed outright will endure frightful suffering, such a use would contravene the ban on weapons that cause superfluous pain. Even the neutron bomb, which the United States claims is a 'tactical' weapon capable of hitting only limited objectives (its effect being mainly one of radiation, not of flames and heat), causes horrific suffering in those who are not lucky enough to die at once (according to one's distance from the epicentre, the symptoms are: nausea, vomiting, a change in the composition of blood corpuscles, damage to the nervous system causing convulsions, violent spasms of pain, ataxy and lethargy; otherwise the effects are felt years after one has been exposed to the radiation, in the form of cancer of the lungs or stomach, or tumours of the thyroid gland).[6]

To sum up, the first use of nuclear weapons is indeed prohibited by these two general principles of the law of war. Despite the fact that they crystallized between the seventeenth and nineteenth century, long before the invention of sophisticated weapons, they are so all-embracing as to cover the use of ultra-modern military weapons such as nuclear bombs.

The attitude of nuclear powers before the 60s

Although the two general bans certainly do prohibit the first use of a nuclear bomb, let us now apply ourselves with great *realism* to another problem. Have *nuclear states* succeeded in *undermining* those principles or, to be more precise, have they agreed to consider them inapplicable to nuclear weapons?

What has been the attitude of nuclear powers since 1945?

Let us begin with the bombing of Hiroshima and Nagasaki. The various written records prove that the United States considered that lawful, and continues to do so for the reasons I discussed and criticized in a previous essay. If we are to go by

Churchill's declarations, Great Britain adopted the same attitude. We know nothing of the views of France and communist China (which only came into being in 1949). As for the USSR, it certainly seemed to consider the bombing a contravention of international law, at least according to what an eminent Soviet jurist, E. Korowin, wrote in 1955. He stated repeatedly that, in devastating Hiroshima and Nagasaki, the United States violated both the principles I mentioned earlier.[7]

After 1945 it is worth drawing a distinction between the declarations and statements of states, on the one hand, and the negotiations and debates in the United Nations, on the other.

As for the first, both the United States and Great Britain stood firmly by their original 1945 attitudes. Both nations wrote into their military manuals (a collection of regulations, binding on their armed forces) that the use of nuclear weapons 'as such' is not banned by the existing rules. Besides, the manuals of the US Navy and Air Force added that to use such a weapon 'against military targets' was undoubtedly permissible.[8] There is no documentary evidence of the French attitude on this point. It is reasonable to assume the French hold substantially similar views to the other two major Western powers.

On the other hand, the USSR does not appear to have changed its views, at least not immediately after Hiroshima and Nagasaki. It is worth noting, however, that in an interview published in the *New York Times* on 8 September 1961 Nikita Khrushchev (then head of the government and party secretary), asked if the USSR would use the nuclear bomb first in a war, said

> if either side should in such a war feel it was losing, would it not use nuclear weapons to avoid defeat? It would undoubtedly use its nuclear bombs . . .

In the same period, Khrushchev also declared that the USSR was ready to sign an international agreement in which all states renounced the first use of nuclear weapons. It would thus appear that, in the early 1960s, the Soviet Union, knowing full well what attitude to expect from the Western nuclear powers, was about to change its own attitude in the more realistic search for a specific agreement on the issue.

It is quite impossible to decide what the Chinese government's attitude was, at least until the 1970s.

The 1961 debate in the United Nations

The showdown came when a group of Third World countries (Ceylon, Ethiopia, Ghana, Guinea, Indonesia, Liberia, Libya, Nigeria, Somalia, Sudan, Togo, Tunisia) presented a draft resolution in 1961 at the United Nations. Without mincing words, the resolution proclaimed that the use of nuclear and thermonuclear weapons was prohibited by the UN Charter and by general international law, in any circumstances whatsoever (even in retaliation to a nuclear attack). This was because 'it would exceed even the scope of war and cause indiscriminate suffering and destruction to mankind and civilization'. The resolution also suggested that a special conference might be held in which all the participants signed a convention on the prohibition of nuclear and thermonuclear arms. Obviously, the twelve Third World countries wanted the convention to *reiterate*, in solemn terms and with binding force, the ban which they felt was already contained in the Charter and in international law.

The Soviet Union immediately supported the resolution, whereas, led by the United States, the Western countries criticized it on three separate counts. First, the ban was devoid of any credibility or force, because an effective ban on the use of nuclear weapons could not be derived from UN resolutions, but had to be negotiated in a multinational conference on disarmament. Second, the resolution contained no guarantee against its violation by the USSR – the Western states felt the Soviet Union had no real intention of respecting the ban – but was entirely inspired by motives of political propaganda. Third, the resolution was defective in that it did not mention the possibility of using nuclear arms in *self-defence* (that is, to repulse the nuclear attack of another country) as laid down in article 51 of the UN Charter. Despite this plain-spoken criticism, the Western nations were ready to reach a compromise, so long as the idea of self-defence was upheld. To this effect Italy, with the backing of the other Western states, suggested certain amendments that would make allowance for the right to self-defence.

However, both the twelve Afro-Asian states and the USSR refused to budge and the Italian amendments were rejected – even though the Western states had promised to support the resolution as a whole if these amendments had been accepted. The resolution was approved by 55 votes in favour (including that of the USSR), 20 votes against (Western states, including the United States, the United Kingdom and France) and 26 abstentions.[9] It was a Pyrrhic victory.

What can be said of this first political and diplomatic 'skirmish'? An important opportunity was lost because of the obdurate refusal, quite unjustified in retrospect, of the USSR and the Third World countries to accept the Western amendments which, to a large extent, were entirely justified. Anyone reading an account of the 1961 debate today is left with the impression that the Third World countries acted with very little sense of realism. They seem to have held a naive faith in the magical power of words – as if a majority vote for the resolution meant that the Western nations were then bound to respect the ban it contained. One also gets the impression that the West was right to feel that Soviet approval was inspired more by reasons of propaganda, especially with regard to the Third World. This seems to be clearly discernible in Soviet (and Third World) declarations rejecting the Italian amendments on self-defence. Had they been more realistic and constructive, both the Soviet Union and the Third World nations could have accepted those amendments, as long as it was clear that 'self-defence' meant the reaction to an armed attack already in progress, not 'pre-emptive' self-defence. In other words, these states could have seized the opportunity to erase the ambiguity intrinsic to the idea of 'self-defence' as contained in the Western proposal. (As I have already mentioned in another essay, Western nations more than any other group hold that self-defence, as described in article 51 of the UN Charter, includes the use of force when it is *believed* that an enemy attack is imminent. This is a particularly broad loophole in the ban on the use of force.) The USSR and the Third World states could have insisted that the West explicitly rule out 'pre-emptive' self-defence. (It is more than likely that the Soviet delegates in New York were well aware of the Western proposal's political and military implications: if they rejected it *in toto* without suggesting constructive alternatives, it was for transparent political and military reasons of their own.) The most likely conjecture is that a total ban on the use of nuclear weapons would have handed the military advantage over to the

USSR, because it then had – and still has – the upper hand as far as conventional weapons (including chemical weapons) are concerned. Once nuclear weapons had been 'frozen' and their use rigorously banned by universal agreement, obviously the state with most conventional arms could win a future full-scale war.

All the 1961 resolution did was to drop a bucket into a dry well and each of the nuclear states maintained its original position (except the USSR, which now found itself in a state of contradiction, if one compares the Soviet vote for the resolution with Khrushchev's declarations to the *New York Times*).

A turning point: the early 1970s

The USSR reiterated its acceptance of a total prohibition in 1972, when it championed a ban on any use whatsoever (first use, second, third, etc.) of nuclear weapons in the UN General Assembly. On this occasion Western states were highly critical and even Third World countries did not seem enthusiastic, at first. To dispel their doubts, the USSR consented to a modification of the resolution for the purpose of upholding 'the principle of the inadmissibility of acquisition of territory by force and the inherent right of states to recover such territories by all the means at their disposal' (clearly this was a reference, requested by the Arab states, to their rights over the territories occupied by Israel). The USSR then made another concession: it accepted a reference to self-defence which, however, rendered the scope of the resolution contradictory and ambiguous. Thus distorted, the resolution was finally approved by 73 votes in favour and 4 against (including China) and 46 abstentions (among these the Western nuclear powers).[10] Once again, an attempt to reach an agreement in the United Nations *reiterating* the traditional ban on the first strike ended in failure, further proof of the USSR's equivocal position and the West's firm opposition to a ban that did not include negotiations on disarmament in general.

After this second set-back, a new period begins during which China's position is given clearer definition, that of the West remains unchanged and the Soviet attitude is transformed.

First, let us take a quick look at the Chinese position. This was defined in 1972 by Peking's delegate to the General Assembly and confirmed repeatedly there and in other international forums over the next few years. China felt that the nuclear powers should pledge themselves never to use nuclear weapons first, either among themselves or against non-nuclear states. China also promised solemnly never to use nuclear weapons first against non-nuclear nations; it later undertook – or so it would seem – never to use them first against any other nuclear state.[11] This seems to prove that it did not consider their first use banned as yet. A unilateral pledge of this kind would have been superfluous had nuclear weapons already been banned by international law.

In 1978 the Soviet Union contradicted what it had said up till then when it abstained on a resolution, proposed by the Third World countries in the United Nations, declaring nuclear weapons contrary to international law. The official reason for the new Soviet attitude was that the resolution artificially separated the issue of nuclear weapons both from that of the measures to be adopted to improve international security and from that of the non-use of force in general.[12] Then, in 1982, Gromyko told the General Assembly that the Soviet Union solemnly and unilaterally pledged itself never to use nuclear weapons first.[13] Furthermore, in 1983 a Soviet scholar wrote in an official magazine of his native country that no international rules yet exist which 'explicitly' ban the use of nuclear arms; he, therefore, urged that all states follow the Soviet example and make solemn declarations that they will never use these weapons first.[14]

All these elements go to prove that the Soviet Union changed its attitude radically at the end of the 1970s. It now believes that the first use of nuclear weapons *is not banned* by the current general rules of international law. Let me add that in 1975 the Soviet Union had already adopted an interesting stance along these lines at the Geneva Diplomatic Conference on the Humanitarian Law of Armed Conflict. On that occasion it agreed with major Western powers (the United States, the United Kingdom and France) that the rules they were drafting would not touch on nuclear arms. In other words, the USSR felt the political climate was not inclined to include nuclear weapons within the scope of the bans under discussion (the Conference culminated in the approval of a Protocol, in 1977, which, among other points, was intended to protect the civilian population from indiscriminate attack).[15]

It is not easy to perceive the precise reasons for the new Soviet attitude. The USSR probably realized that, given the stance adopted by other nuclear powers, it would have been unrealistic to go on asserting that the first use of nuclear arms was already prohibited. Perhaps it felt that, from a political point of view, it was more constructive to start from the assumption that the first strike was lawful, and then seek to negotiate a ban to which all nations would agree.

A rapid glance at the Great Powers' position today

As we have seen, from the very first the three Western nuclear states held that the first use of nuclear weapons was not contrary to international law. In other words, in their opinion it is lawful to use nuclear arms in two cases: either to prevent an imminent attack (whether the aggressor intended to use nuclear or conventional weapons), or in response to an attack by a socialist state, if the enemy uses such arms as can only be counteracted by the use of nuclear weapons. This *legal approach* is in line with the strategic interests of Western states.

China's position is substantially similar; the only difference being that it has solemnly sworn never to use nuclear arms first against other states (whether nuclear or non-nuclear). Thus, China does not believe itself to be bound by an existing *general* international ban on the first use of nuclear arms, either.

Lastly, the Soviet Union now believes there are no international bans on the use of these weapons, but, like China, it has sworn *unilaterally* not to use them first (though the commitment seems to be of greater political than legal value). The underlying supposition is that the duty undertaken by the USSR is entirely dependent on its pledge and not on pre-existing international rules.

Thus, today the five major powers have taken very similar stances on what they believe to be the legitimacy of first use of nuclear weapons in international law. I shall shortly describe the impact of this unanimity on pre-existing law. First, let me underscore a point that is particularly important. Despite their recent concurrence on the use of nuclear arms, all five major powers continue to 'believe' in and feel bound by their commitment *not to use force* (undertaken in 1945 in San Francisco), that is not to attack one another nor to attack other states. In other words, their concurrence on nuclear arms should be seen within the wider framework of the prohibition on aggression, which they all continue to proclaim. They still feel they are legally entitled to use nuclear arms first, but only as the victims of an aggression, whether in *reaction* against one that has already begun (using conventional arms), or to *prevent* a serious and imminent attack (either with conventional or nuclear weapons).

Taking stock

Given this state of affairs, what can be deduced about the present situation? The major powers continue to proclaim the general bans on *resort to force*; though on closer examination these bans are more 'permissive' than they seem. Let us concentrate now on the legal imperatives governing the use of arms.

It is beyond doubt that the bans that can be derived from the two general principles I described earlier also include the first strike with nuclear arms. However, since the five major nuclear powers do not accept this point, can it be said that they have reached a tacit agreement among themselves to the effect that these bans do not include nuclear weapons? I think the answer is yes. The Big Five have concluded a tacit *agreement*, recognizing an *exception* to the two general principles, a kind of *conventio ad excludendum* (which, from a moral point of view, some might call a *pactum sceleris*). By this agreement, they now feel free, in their mutual relations, not to observe the dictates of the two general principles. Naturally this agreement includes certain non-nuclear states that are allied to one or other of the two Great Powers (for example, West Germany).

This leads us to another problem: what value does such a tacit agreement hold for other states, of which most believe that the bans do cover nuclear weapons as well?

At this point, our voyage of exploration founders on one of the most insidious rocks in the sea of the international community: the formal equality of sovereign states, and its corollary, consent. The principle of consent allows two or more states to agree among themselves on exceptions to or derogations from general rules or bans – except in certain specific cases (as foreseen in *jus cogens*), which do not include the one we are discussing here. In our case, formal equality – which in the international community has always served to strengthen and confirm the substantial inequality of nations, all to the advantage of the major powers – has been a useful pawn in the game played by the Great Powers because it offers legal protection to their convergent interests. The majority of non-nuclear states feel that, from the legal point of view, the first use of nuclear weapons *is* unlawful, whether they are used against a non-nuclear state that would not and could not retaliate in kind, or against another nuclear power (because these arms produce effects that sweep across the barriers of time and space, affecting countries other than the enemy's).

This dichotomy places states in a *terrible predicament*: although most non-nuclear states consider the use of nuclear arms prohibited and therefore unlawful, the five major nuclear powers have agreed among themselves, together with certain other states that are their political and military allies, that their use is lawful. (However, it is necessary to point out that the USSR and China, by their unilateral declarations, would appear to stand apart from other nuclear powers, though it is *dubious how binding* these pledges are; besides, the unilateral declarations do nothing to remove the two states' conviction that *according to international law* to use nuclear weapons is *not to violate* the general principles we have been discussing.) Consequently, if one of the Great Powers launches a nuclear attack on another – or on its ally – the use of nuclear weapons between the warring parties *is not unlawful*, whereas it *is unlawful* for third states (whether or not they have been affected in some way by the destructive force of those weapons). Thus, the same action is *lawful* for a few, but *strictly forbidden* for the many. At this point, law has no more to say on the matter. If its function is to regulate and curb dangerous actions, in this case it is quite impotent, because its bans are fully recognized only by states that do not possess nuclear weapons and therefore do not need to be guided and constrained in such matters. The relevant law indeed exists and its rules have been laid down, but these rules are impotent because they are *ineffectual against the powerful states*, the only ones who ought to heed them: they have been checkmated by the 'agreement to derogate' from the ban on nuclear arms. For the nuclear powers, therefore, law exists only in the guise of a *permissive* set of rules.

In theory, at least, the nuclear powers *should* respect the two general principles as far as non-nuclear states are concerned, if only because the latter firmly believe those principles to be applicable to nuclear weapons. But how can one force the former to respect the principles when they have the whip hand? Since the international community has no institutional mechanism for applying sanctions, this is an area in which the feebleness of legal imperatives is felt to be more devastating than elsewhere.

We must draw the bitter conclusion that the two general bans – embodying the basic needs of civilized human society and voicing the better instincts of people – are too harmless to be heeded by the powerful states. They merely serve to guide the actions of weak states and shape the opinions of the most right-minded sectors in nuclear states, inducing the latter in the future, perhaps, though probably only gradually, to agree on explicit bans that must be obeyed and can be 'checked'. Today they can be used as yardsticks, from the ethical and political point of view, by which to judge the actions of the major powers, should one or more of them contravene these general bans – always providing it is still possible for ordinary people to express an opinion after a disaster of such colossal proportions.

When faced with the most menacing threat of our time, law does not utter a loud and clear 'yes' or 'no' to the first use of nuclear weapons, as people commonly think it does. Its response is many-faceted, if not downright contradictory. Mere words have been unable to ban the bomb; this is hardly surprising since those very bombs are in the hands of the Great Powers, who know full well how to manipulate legal rules and institutions. Here again law is a two-faced Janus: it supports the strong and allows the Great to use the bomb; yet it suggests that this use would violate the most elementary humanitarian imperatives and offers guidelines by which non-nuclear states (those that have not abjectly followed the lead of the Great) can condemn the first use of nuclear arms as unlawful. Thus, law supports the 'Prince', but is not totally deaf to the voices of the many who may perish by the 'Prince's sword'.

Of nuclear weapons it has been said that, in our present world, they are the opposite of bayonets, described in the nineteenth century as good for all purposes but no use as a shooting-stick. If, so far, a catastrophe of world proportions has been avoided, it is because the military have merely sat upon their bombs. Yet, they are as dangerous as ever. That is why jurists and diplomats, with the full support of public opinion, now face the Sisyphean task of convincing politicians and the military to do their utmost to ensure that mankind may, sooner or later, sit around the conference table without the fear of being blown to smithereens.

4

Negotiation Versus Force
The *Achille Lauro* imbroglio

An exemplary 'incident'

In an ocean of violence, in which people are faced with ever increasing perils, the *Achille Lauro* affair is less remarkable for what actually happened than for the new trends in international relations it revealed. The case is exemplary, in more senses than one. It shows how fragile the thread of our lives is, since even a pleasure cruise is fraught with danger that can spill over, at any moment, from current political violence. It illustrates how, when (more or less) private groups commit an outrage, they can provoke sovereign states to similar acts of armed violence. It shows that the political protocols are neglected in favour of the rough and ready use of force both by groups and states. Finally, it is an example of how intricately intertwined human relations are: the ship was Italian, the passengers were of diverse nationalities, the terrorists were Palestinian and the incident involved several nations (Egypt, Italy, the United States and, to a lesser extent, West Germany). Besides, news of the hijack was transmitted to the world, at 2 p.m. on 7 October 1985, by a radio station in Göteborg in Sweden.

The facts

On 7 October 1985, four gunmen belonging to one of the PLO factions (the Palestine Liberation Front or PLF, which is itself divided into three subgroups), hijacked the Italian transatlantic liner, the *Achille Lauro* at roughly twenty-seven sea miles from

Port Said, where it was sailing *en route* from Alexandria, with 201 passengers (including Swiss, Austrians, Italians, Americans and Germans) enjoying a pleasure cruise, and a crew of 344 (Italians and Portuguese). Apparently, the original plan was for the terrorists to land, mingling with the crowd of passengers, at the Israeli port of Ashod and to carry out a massacre there. However, fearing they might be detected while still at sea and arrested on landing, the gunmen hijacked the whole ship and held the passengers hostage, threatening to kill the Americans and the British unless Israel freed fifty Palestinians from their prisons. The Syrians subsequently refused them entry into the port of Tartous and, having sailed up and down the eastern Mediterranean, the hijackers started to negotiate with Abu Abbas, an intermediary sent by Arafat to Egypt. The upshot was an agreement with Egypt, backed by Italy and West Germany – that the terrorists were not to spill a drop of blood of their hostages and were to surrender on the understanding that they would not be prosecuted and would be allowed to depart for Tunisia (where the PLO has its headquarters). On 10 October, when they disembarked at Port Said, no one knew how many terrorists there were, nor whether any of the hostages had been killed. Once the gunmen had left the liner, the captain spoke via radio to the Italian Prime Minister, Bettino Craxi, and told him that an American citizen (only later did the news come that this was Leon Klinghoffer) had been murdered. However, the Egyptians denied they knew anything about the killing and, on October 10 at 9.30 p.m., the gunmen were allowed to leave for Tunis, with Abu Abbas and another Palestinian leader, five Eygptian diplomats and ten armed guards, also Egyptian, on an Egyptian aircraft 'used for public purposes'. That night the Tunisians refused to let the aeroplane land. After trying to land in Greece, it was flying back to Egypt when four US jets from the *Saratoga* aircraft carrier intercepted it and forced it to follow them and land at the military base of Sigonella (in Sicily), where NATO units of the American army are stationed. The plane touched down at the same time as two US C141 military transport planes and it was immediately surrounded by Italian soldiers, themselves encircled by US special troops (the Delta force) under orders to take the hijackers and the members of the PLO to the US transport planes. But the Italian soldiers prevented this tug-of-war. What followed was between Italy and the United States. In the end, with a nod of approval from the Egyptian government, the four hijackers were taken prisoner by the Italian police, and the two PLO leaders remained aboard the Egyptian aircraft. However, the Egyptians allowed the Italian Prime Minister Bettino Craxi's diplomatic adviser to board the plane and 'take a statement' from Abu Abbas. On the morning of 11 October, the aeroplane, with the two members of the PLO and the Egyptians, flew towards Rome, escorted by four Italian jet fighters and tailed by an American jet which had no permission to overfly Italian territory. At Ciampino airport in Rome, another US military aircraft taxied up beside the Egyptian plane and 'declared a state of emergency'. The US government then urged its Italian counterpart to hand over Abu Abbas. The negotiations, at this stage, involved Italy, the Palestinians and Egypt (the latter held a trump card: the *Achille Lauro* was still in Egyptian territorial waters and would only be allowed to set sail after the Italians had released the Egyptian aircraft). Finally, Abu Abbas, who 'was protected by the diplomatic immunity granted him by the Republic of Iraq',[1] and the other member of the PLO, were allowed to leave for Yugoslavia; they subsequently disappeared without trace.

The behaviour of the Americans was so provocative that both Egypt and Italy sent notes of protest to Washington. The former objected to the 'illegal' hijacking of its aeroplane; the latter to the violation of Italian airspace by an American military aircraft. The Americans themselves thought they had not received the co-operation they felt was their due. Roughly a year later, the case before the Court of Assizes in Genoa ended with heavy sentences for the hijackers and a life sentence for Abu Abbas and for two other instigators of the kidnapping (themselves fugitives from justice, like Abu Abbas). Nevertheless, these hefty penalties were greeted with ill-tempered resentment in America, where the public expressed its indignation at the 'indulgence' of the Italian judges and for the excessive 'courtesy' the Italian government had shown Abu Abbas while he was in Italy.

These are the main points of an intricate episode, part thriller, part western, with elements of diplomatic intrigue and scenes from a war film thrown in. I shall endeavour to unravel the main knots in this cat's-cradle gone wrong, especially from the legal and political points of view, to see how they got that way and whether alternative solutions would have produced fewer tangles.

The agreement to let the terrorists go free

It is fairly obvious that the hijackers were not acting on orders from a state, or even for the PLO, but merely for one faction of that organization, the PLF. This hijack, which was not a case of *piracy* proper (since the gunmen did not act for private ends, but in the pursuit of political objectives), could not be put at the door of any subject of international law. This made the negotiations more complicated. Sovereign states and national liberation movements with a minimum of legitimacy and recognition from the international community can sit round a negotiating table, but this becomes far more awkward if the counterpart is an organization that practises terrorism. It is difficult enough to negotiate, let alone reach an agreement, with such as these. This explains why both Italy and Egypt wanted Arafat's collaboration, and why Egypt allowed Abu Abbas (who at the time seemed to be acting for the Chairman of the PLO) to come to Cairo to persuade the kidnappers to hand over the ship.

A written agreement for the 'liberation of the terrorists' was reached between the Egyptian government and Abu Abbas on 8 October 1985. It merely stated that

> the groups responsible for the action against the Italian ship *Achille Lauro* have to surrender immediately on the following conditions:
> i.   no request to be presented for their extradition or prosecution;
> ii. the PLO will take them in charge.

The agreement did not mention as a condition that the hijackers must not have killed anyone, nor committed any act of violence while aboard the liner; however, according to Mubarak, Craxi and Andreotti, this condition was implicit. The text of the agreement was shown by the Egyptian Foreign Minister to the ambassadors of Italy, the United States, Great Britain and West Germany, but only the Italian and German ambassadors countersigned it, after consulting their respective foreign ministers. Thus the three signatory states had undertaken not to prosecute the hijackers and Egypt had further consented to allow the gunmen to leave for the PLO headquarters in Tunisia.

It is not clear why Egypt pretended to know nothing about the killing of a passenger on board the liner and decided to uphold their side of the agreement, allowing the terrorists and Abu Abbas to leave their country on an Egyptian official aircraft.

Whatever its reasons, Egypt had certainly ratified (together with the United States) the 1979 Convention on the taking of hostages. Article 5 of this Convention (to which Italy was not a party), obliged Egypt to prosecute the hijackers, that is if it did not want to extradite them to the United States (Klinghoffer was a US citizen). This explains why the American ambassador did not countersign the agreement to give the terrorists a safe conduct; without the United States' countersignature the agreement had no validity whatsoever for the Americans. By not prosecuting the terrorists and not handing them over to the Americans, the Egyptians had broken their obligation under the Convention on hostages.

Undoubtedly, Egypt faced a dreadful dilemma; if it respected its obligations towards the United States (and other countries that were party to the Convention) it risked the violent reactions of Abu Abbas's group of terrorists, as well as a worsening of relations with the Palestinians, already fairly tense; otherwise, it could circumvent the obligations of the Convention in various ways (for example, by handing the hijackers to Arafat, who had promised to prosecute them himself: a move which, to some extent, seemed to provide for their incrimination). In fact, from the point of view of international law, Egypt should have prosecuted the terrorists itself, or extradited them to another sovereign state which was also a party to the Convention – never to an organization that many states, including the United States, did not recognize. In weighing the pros and the cons, Egypt decided that to infringe the rules of the Convention was a lesser evil than the political and diplomatic consequences of a crisis in its relations with the Palestinians.

The use of force by the United States

Once the US government discovered that the gunmen and Abu Abbas had boarded a plane in Cairo, it decided to intercept the aircraft; and so it did, after it had been turned away by Tunisia and

Greece and was probably flying back to Cairo. The United States later behaved in a high-handed manner with Italy too, when it ordered one of their military planes to overfly Italian territory (from Sigonella to Rome) without the necessary authorization. By so doing, the United States certainly violated Italian territorial sovereignty (and Craxi promptly sent Washington a note of protest) and behaved in shallow and overbearing manner. (What was the point of irritating a faithful ally? What use was it to pursue the Egyptian jet, since they could hardly intercept it in Italian airspace?) However, the violation of Italian airspace was probably more a case of political simple-mindedness than of the deliberate waiving of international law.

Leaving aside the question of Italian territorial sovereignty, let us turn to the intercepting of the Egyptian jet. This was 'hijacked' by American jet fighters just before midnight (Italian time) on 10 October and forced to land at Sigonella. In his speech to the Chamber of Deputies, on 17 October, Craxi said the jet 'was on a special mission for the Egyptian government and therefore enjoyed extraterritoriality'.[2] In any case, even if it had not been on a special mission, but merely on a normal passenger flight, the interception would still have violated international law, especially article 2, paragraph 4 of the UN Charter, which prohibits the threat of use or force.

Was there any legal justification for the interception? Neither the idea of reprisal, nor that of self-defence apply in this case. *Armed reprisals* are prohibited under international law beyond any shadow of doubt. When Egypt omitted to observe the 1979 Convention, the United States could not react with force, but only with some countermeasure of a peaceful nature. Nor could the United States invoke *self-defence*, since this is the reaction to an armed attack (and, in the view of some, the prevention of such an attack). In the case of the *Achille Lauro*, Egypt could not be held to have either planned or carried out an armed attack.

The Americans never offered any formal justification for their behaviour, feeling that they were right to act as they did. So much so, that Reagan later refused Mubarak's request for public excuses (which is the least he could have done). However, before the jet was intercepted, during a discussion in the UN Security Council on the Middle Eastern crisis, the

American delegate suggested a justification that is worth examining. His reasoning went as follows: for centuries pirates were considered the 'common enemies of all mankind' because they endangered navigation and robbed and murdered people; for centuries the international community allowed any state, even states that had not been the victims of direct attack from pirates, to capture and punish the criminals; since terrorism is the *modern equivalent of piracy*, terrorists are the 'enemies of us all'.

> The terrorist has put himself beyond the reach of civilized humanity. He should be shunned by all. If he seeks sanctuary he should be turned away. If he claims support he should be denounced. If he is apprehended he should be prosecuted. Every terrorist attack is an attack on the world community. Every justification offered for terrorism undermines the rule of law. Every concession to the terrorists diminishes our humanity.[3]

I feel that these words, as well as those of President Reagan's spokesman after the jet was intercepted,[4] reveal a clear line of policy, even if it is not explicitly mentioned: the terrorist is the pirate of modern times and, in fighting terrorists, states enjoy the same powers as were granted to those that had to deal with piracy. The US government was acting in the interests of justice, to ensure that odious crimes, such as injure all mankind, were punished.

This argument is unacceptable (perhaps this explains why the State Department never used it officially). First, before the analogy with piracy is accepted as valid it must be 'authorized' in clear and explicit terms by the international community in the form of a general rule; but no such rule exists as yet, despite a widespread rumbling of disapproval of terrorism. Certain and irrefutable proof that such a rule exists must be put forward, because it would in fact be a second exception to article 2, paragraph 4 of the UN Charter banning the use of force, the first being that of self-defence (article 51 of the Charter).

The American 'theory' should be rejected on other grounds as well. The old rule on piracy, *juris gentium*, allowed states to use force against *individuals* (the pirates) and their vessels. In our case the United States used force against a *state* aircraft that was transporting the hijackers. This would not have been allowed by the old international rule even in the case of real pirates. Finally, one can also argue that the American analogy is untenable because of the negative effects of an 'authorization' to use force in political and diplomatic relations between states. If today international relations are in a state of semi-anarchy, such an 'authorization' would make them totally anarchic: the Great Powers and some middle-sized ones, too, would feel they could legitimately use force against foreigners – whom they chose to call 'terrorists' – wherever they might be. This would lead to ever increasing tension and conflict between the 'police' states and the countries to which these individuals belonged.

Above all, the US theory would not only legitimize the use of force against *states* that finance, organize and command groups of terrorists (because then those states could be accused directly of fostering acts of terrorism), it would also legitimize the use of force in far more tenuous cases of 'involvement', such as that of Egypt in the *Achille Lauro* affair. To comprehend the colossal gap between the American theory and current international law, one should remember how the international community reacted to cases of violence by states against *individuals* living abroad (i.e. the kidnapping of Eichmann by Israeli agents in Argentina): in such cases, the international community has already condemned the use of force against individuals, when this has not been authorized by the territorial state. All the more reason why the international community would feel obliged to condemn the use of (unauthorized) force against a *state* (no matter where this takes place, whether on state territory or in international airspace).

Let me add that the use of force by 'police' states would lead to an escalation of violence, because it would provoke the terrorists to acts of ever increasing barbarity against an ever greater number of innocent victims.

What makes it even harder to understand the motives behind the American behaviour in the *Achille Lauro* case is that reasonable and peaceful alternatives did exist, capable of producing the same results. The Americans already knew from Craxi that 'Italy intended to ask Egypt to extradite the four hijackers so as to subject them to the due process of law in Italy.' They also knew that, 'should the hijackers, meanwhile, be transferred to PLO custody', the Italian government had already decided to ask that Organization to hand them over. While the Italian Foreign Minister was about to instruct the

Italian ambassador in Tunis to this effect, Craxi had 'sent Yasser Arafat a request to deliver them to Italy'. Thus, the United States intercepted the Egyptian jet knowing full well that the appropriate measures to bring the terrorists to justice were about to be taken. Worse still, the plane was intercepted when it was looking for somewhere to land and was probably heading for Egypt. The latter had undertaken at an international level to punish or extradite any kidnappers. Once the plane had landed, the Egyptian government *could no longer have ignored its commitments under the 1979 Convention.* Indeed, at that stage Egypt could no longer pretend to be unaware of Klinghoffer's assassination. The seriousness of the crime and the strong diplomatic pressures both of the United States and of other countries, including Italy, were likely to make political expediency give way to respect for legal obligations. The United States would have held the trump card and could have played it without infringing the rules of the international community and injuring the prestige of a political ally in the Mediterranean.

In this case, international law did offer valid and expedient alternatives to the use of force. The United States preferred violence, with regrettable consequences for the rule of law in general and also for the political and diplomatic relations in the area. A dangerous precedent was set (encouraging the Great Powers and other states to do likewise in the future); besides, the sovereign rights, as well as the prestige, of two faithful allies were trodden underfoot. 'Emotion' was allowed to prevail over 'reason', with negative results all round. As far as the United States was concerned, the cost to benefits ratio was disastrous.

The part played by Italy

There has been considerable criticism and bewilderment about the behaviour of the Italian authorities, both in Italy and abroad. I would like, here, to take a look at the legal and political aspects of the case, in so far as the available evidence allows.

No one can doubt that the decision to waive prosecution and extradition of the hijackers, as it was expressed in the Cairo agreement, was legal and dictated by laudable motives of political opportunity. Assuming that the hijackers had not drawn blood and in the hope that they would immediately free their 545 hostages, the Italian government was entitled to waive the right to request the arrest and punishment of the gunmen who had captured the Italian liner. Nor is there any doubt (as the statements of Craxi's diplomatic adviser confirm)[5] that, when the agreement was signed by the Italian ambassador in Cairo, Italy knew nothing of Klinghoffer's murder.

Furthermore, Italy was entirely within the law and was trying its utmost to reach a negotiated agreement when the government, on learning of Klinghoffer's death, immediately decided to send a request for the extradition of the hijackers both to Egypt and to the PLO (in case the terrorists were entrusted by Egypt to the latter's custody).

Besides, Italy's third decision was, I feel, fully legitimate when, after the Egyptian jet had landed at Sigonella, the government showed its determination not to extradite the four hijackers to the United States. Indeed, article 3 of the bilateral agreement on extradition of 13 October 1983 states that 'when an offense has been committed outside the territory' of either party, the requested party can decide whether or not to grant the request. Since the crime was committed on the high seas on an Italian ship, the Italian government had every right to refuse extradition; proof of the gunmen's guilt was all that was needed for Italian courts to have jurisdiction over the matter.

However, this was not the bone of contention. What the Americans have criticized so bitterly is what they call Italy's pusillanimous resort to *raisons d'état*. They say they had ample proof of Abu Abbas's guilt; they could show he had masterminded the whole affair, that he had not just directed the operation from the moment the terrorists decided to hijack the liner instead of carrying out their intended massacre in Israel. Italy advanced three distinct reasons why it did not wish to proceed to the 'provisional arrest' of Abu Abbas requested by the United States. First, it considered the proof of the Palestinian leader's criminal activities, as put forward by the Americans, very tenuous. Here we have nothing to go on but the discretionary evaluation of the Italian government (which had submitted the American 'evidence' to the independent assessment of three Italian judges). Second, the Egyptian plane was 'on a special mission for the Egyptian government' and, therefore, enjoyed extra-territorial rights (the Italians could not board the aircraft and arrest Abu Abbas without the explicit consent of its captain). This argument is technically valid. However, if the Italian government really intended to allow an Italian judge to question the Palestinian, they could have negotiated to that effect with the Egyptians. It was a situation of stalemate: the Italian police could not arrest Abu Abbas, but the plane could not take off without the consent of the airport authorities. Admittedly, the Egyptians had blocked the departure of the *Achille Lauro* from Port Said; though, of course, the passengers and crew had not much to fear from the authorities of a friendly state that was in the midst of diplomatic negotiations with Italy. However complex and delicate these negotiations, in the end the Egyptians might have allowed an Italian judge at least to question Abu Abbas. Although, unfortunately, Italy was not a party to the Convention of 1979 on the taking of hostages (which it only signed in 1980, and ratified in 1986), it could have reminded Egypt that, under Italian law, a crime committed on the high seas on board an Italian ship must be punished in Italy, and this rule covers both the criminals themselves and their accomplices. One gets the impression that the decision to leave Abu Abbas well alone was only motivated by a desire to avoid future complications with the terrorist group and to 'get back' the *Achille Lauro* without delay, not by a firm resolution to discover whether the Palestinian had masterminded, or was involved in, the incident.

This impression is also supported by the third argument advanced by Italy: that Abu Abbas had declared he enjoyed diplomatic immunity because he possessed an Iraqi diplomatic passport. A very thin argument indeed! There was no supporting proof that he had acted, or was acting, *for Iraq*. The mere possession of a diplomatic passport – given the sophisticated systems used by terrorist groups to get both arms and 'camouflage' documents – should not have been an insurmountable obstacle.

In a final analysis, one might say that Italy constantly avoided taking violent measures but, in the last phase of the affair, it put political opportunity before justice. The fact that the Court of Assizes in Genoa condemned Abu Abbas to life imprisonment a year later only goes to prove that at least his interrogation would have been absolutely justified.

The 'lesson' to be drawn from the incident

Let me conclude with four remarks of a general nature.

First, in the dilemma of choosing between *force* and *law* (that is military coercion or diplomatic negotiation), the United States preferred to use force, whereas Egypt and Italy preferred patient but exhausting bargaining. From the very beginning, the United States told Craxi that it was 'totally against . . . undertaking any negotiation'. The Americans then proceeded to violate the sovereign rights of Egypt and Italy. Worse still, they used force against Egypt without the faintest regard for the rules of civilized interstate relations. However, although Italy and Egypt preferred to negotiate, this *does not mean that they respected the rules of international law to the letter*. As I remarked earlier, Egypt did not abide by the 1979 Convention on the taking of hostages as far as the United States was concerned. Besides, though Italy never actually violated international law, at the eleventh hour its actions were opportunist, to say the least.

Second, on the matter of whether or not to respect the law, let us ask ourselves *which 'paid off' better?* In my opinion, by violating international law the United States was the loser, both from a political and a diplomatic point of view. America did not succeed in capturing and prosecuting the hijackers, and merely offended and irritated two allies, one a member of NATO. Furthermore, other states – with the obvious exception of Israel – disliked the way the United States handled the affair, fearing that it might create a precedent. In fact, what the Superpower did was to *hijack the hijackers*. It comes as no surprise, then, that the Palestinian representative told the Security Council (11 October 1985) that intercepting the jet was an 'official act of terrorism', an 'act of piracy against a civilian aircraft'.[6] Within a few hours the United States had destroyed its patiently accumulated capital of consensus on the need to fight terrorism, set forth by the President of the Security Council in the name of all fifteen member states, on 9 October.[7] On the whole, violating international law proved to be extremely 'unremunerative' for the United States.

As for Egypt and Italy, they tended to follow Machiavelli's advice: 'the enemy must be petted or extinguished', with the accent on the 'petting'. Here too, the lack of respect for the law can hardly be said to have 'paid off'. Even though the expedients used by Italy avoided retaliatory acts of terrorism (and obtained the immediate release of the *Achille Lauro*), it put a strain both on the coalition of the five parties in the Italian government, and on relations with the United States and other Western countries. Besides, it left the world in doubt whether the Italian government was serious in its pursuit of terrorism *at any level*.

My third remark is that *terrorism has a profoundly negative impact on the international community as a whole*. Not only because it imperils the lives of innocent people, but also because it subverts the 'rules of the game' played between sovereign states. The latter know how to face acts of violence from other states, or from insurgents, and have set up a body of rules to cover such incidents. In the past, when individuals (the pirates *juris gentium*) disturbed international relations, sovereign states banded together and allowed each other to use force against the renegades. But terrorism is a new and explosive phenomenon. Whatever states have done on an international level to fight terrorism (multilateral treaties for the arrest, punishment and extradition of terrorists) has proved inadequate. Terrorism shatters international relations because it forces some states to disregard accepted patterns of behaviour, while inducing others to use subterfuge and other unworthy expedients. *Negotiations* – always to be preferred to other means – often founder on the hidden reefs of terrorism; even states that prefer peaceful solutions are obliged to make ambiguous concessions to reach a dubious compromise. This is partly due to the subversive power of terrorism: states would be well advised to remove as soon as possible the causes that underlie the phenomenon.

Lastly, let us take an unblinking look at international affairs. From the point of view of progress towards better relations throughout the world, sovereign states are not the only 'losers' from the effects of terrorism. Terrorism also has a disastrous impact on emerging groups, the national liberation movements that wish to gain international standing. The *Achille Lauro* affair has been no less a blow for the PLO as for the states involved. Even though Egypt and Italy were in continual contact with the organization, treating it as an equal in their negotiations (Italy was even prepared to request that the PLO 'extradite' the hijackers), the PLO behaved with such ambiguity as to lose most of its credibility. To deny any connection with the hijack, which it condemned in harsh terms, cannot be reconciled with the sending of Abu Abbas, the mastermind behind the incident, to 'negotiate' with the terrorists. The whole episode proves that the best known and most widely 'recognized' national liberation movement *is unable to behave as a valid counterpart in negotiations with sovereign states.* It is too deeply lacerated by internal rifts, its leaders are disturbingly two-faced, and its lack of any national territory or any proper government weakens its bargaining power drastically. Terrorism has proved to be the losing card, even for the most important and accepted stateless 'nation'.

Let us hope the incident will cause statesmen and diplomats, as well as the political and military leaders of national liberation movements, to pause and reflect. Otherwise, it will have served only to give world-wide notoriety to the late lamented Achille Lauro, an Italian ship owner, who certainly possessed commercial flair, but was also known for equivocal political manoeuvrings.

5

Sabra and Shatila

The 'novelty' of the 1982 massacre in two Palestinian camps

It is notorious how ethnic, religious and political hatred has produced more than one massacre of the innocents in the Middle East. Yet what took place in Sabra and Shatila on 16 and 17 September 1982 was not just another of those irrational episodes whose very futility leaves us speechless before the spectacle of so many lives ferociously destroyed. That incident involved Israel, a state with strong democratic leanings and people who are not afraid to voice their indignation. Besides, the international press has always kept an eagle eye on Middle Eastern affairs. As a result of these two factors, the massacre became the subject of an inquiry by an Israeli judicial commission, of a wide ranging investigation conducted by eminent international scholars of diverse nationality, and of a solemn pronouncement by the UN General Assembly. Thus, the outstanding new fact of the massacre was that it not only produced echoes in the hearts of those who follow events in the Middle East with profound anguish, but had reverberations in official organizations, whether national or international. These organizations were asked to express their views on the episode and to condemn the guilty parties. Nothing like that had happened before. Let us hope that the indifference with which similar cases of slaughter have been received by the international community will no longer be tolerated – though subsequent massacres, perpetrated by other factions in the same camps of Sabra and Shatila without provoking the echoes produced in September 1982, leave little room for optimism.

Since authoritative organizations examined and evaluated the facts and then passed judgement, what standards did they follow? The most obvious solution was to apply the legal rules of the international community: the massacre had taken place during the military occupation by one state (Israel) of the territory of another (Lebanon), during military operations that are by their very nature subject to international law. In such cases the legal precepts of the world community – often ambiguous and full of loopholes, because states make sure that they keep a certain room for manoeuvre – are absolutely unequivocal. It is easy to understand why. Other episodes, in many respects similar to Sabra and Shatila, have occurred in recent years; quite a few states have thus been able to express their views, resulting in the formation of fairly precise and rigorous rules. Now, despite the existence of such clear-cut parameters, all three bodies either avoided any reference whatsoever to these rules, or applied them in a surprisingly loose way, or did not draw the conclusions that their application prescribed.

The aim of this brief essay is to show *how* this came about, to ask *why* the various international 'agents' involved did not do what their natural duty seemed to prescribe, and to see *what other standards of behaviour* they applied instead.

The facts

Very briefly, let me just recall the 'facts' on which everyone agreed. During the military occupation of Lebanon by the Israeli armed forces (beginning 6 June 1982, called 'Operation Peace in Galilee'), the Lebanese President, Bechir Gemayel (leader of the Phalangists), was assassinated (14 September) a few days after his election. The Christian (Phalangist) forces attributed the crime to the Palestinians. The Israeli army, fearing a series of awful vendettas, entered West Beirut 'to prevent possible grave occurrences and to ensure quiet'. The Israeli military command, however, allowed the Phalangists to enter the Palestinian camps of Sabra and Shatila to ferret out and arrest any 'Palestinian terrorists' they might find. The Israeli forces surrounded the two camps; according to their orders 'only one element and that is the IDF (Israeli Defence Force), shall command the forces in the area'; in other words, even though only the Phalangists actually entered the two camps, they were operating from the very start of the operation under the aegis and control of the Israelis.

The Christian militias entered the camps on Thursday 16 September at about 6 p.m. A few hours after their entry, an Israeli officer learned from a Phalangist liaison officer that the latter had told one of his soldiers, who had captured forty-five people in one camp and wanted to know what to do with them, 'Do the will of God'. An hour before this conversation, another Israeli officer had distinctly heard (and informed his superiors) a Phalangist officer telling soldiers who had captured fifty women and children in the camps and were awaiting further orders, 'This is the last time you're going to ask me a question like that, you know exactly what to do!' This answer, transmitted via radio to all the forces operating in the camps, was greeted by loud laughter from the Phalangists standing around the officer. Although various Israelis soon realized what a sinister turn the Phalangist operation was taking, and promptly informed their superior officers, or did so in the following hours, the latter did absolutely nothing. Only on Friday evening (17 September), when news of the massacres had spread and even an Israeli journalist had begun to make inquiries, did the Israeli commanding officers start to examine the facts, discovering that the rumours they had heard earlier were quite true. However, the Phalangists were not made to leave the camps, on Israeli orders, until 5 a.m. on Saturday 18 September. The most amazing fact of all is that Prime Minister Begin was not informed until he heard the news on the afternoon of Saturday 18 September, on a BBC broadcast!

These facts, culled from the Israeli Commission of Inquiry's report,[1] prove without question that:

1 The massacre was perpetrated by the Phalangists.
2 The Phalangists entered the Palestinian camps only with the consent and under the eye of the Israeli army.
3 The latter discovered at once that the Phalangists were killing the inhabitants of the camps indiscriminately and did nothing to stop the slaughter.

The Israeli Commission of Inquiry

On 28 September 1982, the pressure of public opinion, both in Israel and abroad, forced Begin to set up a Commisssion of Inquiry, based on an Israeli law of 1968.[2] The same law ensured that the members of the Commission were nominated by the President of the Supreme Court of Israel, Y. Kahan; it included Kahan himself, A. Barak (another Supreme Court judge) and Major General Efrat (Reserve). Given its wide powers of inquiry, the Commission was able to winnow the facts with great care and call numerous witnesses. In its exhaustive report it concluded that various members of the Cabinet and of the Israeli Army were, to varying degrees, 'indirectly responsible'. Among other things, it recommended that the Defence Minister, Ariel Sharon, should be asked to resign (and the Prime Minister was urged to make him do so). The Commission also suggested that the Director of Military Intelligence, Major General Y. Saguy, should be removed from his post and that the Division Commander, Brigadier General A. Yaron, should be suspended for three years.

It is not easy to judge whether the Commission's recommendations, later adopted by the Begin government, were an adequate 'punishment' for Israeli responsibility. But, given the scope of its mandate, it is hard to understand why the Commission did not give a ruling on the responsibilities of the Phalangists and did not suggest what measures the Israeli authorities should adopt to seek out and punish the perpetrators of the massacres. This is a serious shortcoming. However, although the Israeli government was mainly responsible for this failure, the Commission might have given a wider interpretation to its mandate: it could have decided that the mandate empowered it to declare that the Israelis were duty-bound to ensure that those 'directly responsible' were punished, since the latter were still subject to Israeli political and military control.

However, the point I would like to make is another: what parameters did the Commission follow before reaching its 'verdict'?

Briefly, I feel that it should have applied either *Israeli law* (for instance, the 1963 Israeli military manual, *The Laws of War*, that regulates the behaviour of Israeli armed forces during the military occupation of foreign territories, among other things), or *international law*. However, the Commission set both of these bodies of rules aside and referred exclusively to *moral and religious imperatives*. Let us take a look at its reasoning.

First, the Commission drew a distinction between 'direct' and 'indirect' responsibility, without stating from what source (Israeli or international law, ethics or logic) this distinction was drawn. It then observed that only the Phalangists could be held directly responsible. Therefore, as far as the Israelis were concerned, all that remained was to ascertain who had been indirectly responsible. Here the Commission stated that it was not among its tasks to define the legal concept of 'indirect responsibility'. Perhaps from a legal point of view the question was easily resolved, the Commission reported, since the Israeli forces had the status of forces of occupation and, therefore, were charged with public safety. But, it added, even if this status could not be attributed to the Israeli forces, the question of 'indirect responsibility' still remained. At this point it quoted Deuteronomy and the Talmudic interpretation of a passage from that book (the description of the reaction of the sages of a city on discovering the corpse of an unknown man; as quoted by the Commission, the Talmudic interpretation of this episode would prove that, according to the Bible, men are responsible if they witness a crime being committed by others and do nothing either to prevent it, or to help the victim). After this quotation, the Commission invoked the tenets of morality, to which it referred again at the end of its long report.

It is difficult to understand exactly why the Commission shunned the terrain of law. However, we can make a conjecture. The Commission probably kept clear of this path for two reasons. By not adopting a rigorous stand on the legal status of the Israeli occupying troops in Lebanon, it avoided expressing opinions that could have harmed the policy of the Begin Cabinet, which was notorious for having pursued, with regard to the military occupation of Arab territories, a policy that other states (including the United States) could not approve; and even when it occupied Lebanon, it did so for very controversial reasons. Furthermore, in referring to moral and religious principles, it probably intended to underscore these principles and elevate them high above legal ones. The Commission thus followed a line of 'neo-natural' law on the premise that, whatever the dictates of mere human law, there is a Superior Law, which all civilized nations must obey.

The International Commission of Inquiry

On 28 August 1982 a group of private individuals decided to set up an International Commission to examine whether Israel had indeed violated international law by sending its troops into Lebanon on the well-known 'Peace in Galilee' operation. Chaired by Sean MacBride (Nobel Peace prize winner) and made up of five eminent Western scholars, including the international lawyer Professor R. Falk of Princeton University, the Commission also investigated the Sabra and Shatila massacres, even though this task had not been foreseen when it was set up.

The Commission made a thorough inquiry into the facts, also using eye-witness accounts, and concluded that Israel was undoubtedly 'guilty' because: (1) the suspicion of the direct involvement of the Israeli army in the massacre had never been completely disproved; besides, (2) Israel was guilty of grave breaches of international law because its armed forces, duty-bound to maintain order and exercise effective control over the Phalangists, had shielded the Phalangists and helped them to plan and execute the massacre.[3]

This Commission thus based its arguments on international law. However, it referred to rules that Israel does not consider applicable: the Fourth Geneva Convention of 1949 on the Protection of Civilian Populations and the First Geneva Additional Protocol of 1977. The Convention protects the rights of all those who are not citizens of the occupying state (article 4), hence the Palestinians living in Sabra and Shatila, who were either Lebanese, Jordanian or stateless persons. According to some authorities the Convention grants an insufficient protection to those who possess the status of refugees (whatever their nationality);[4] therefore, the majority of the inhabitants of the two camps were only partially covered. Be that as it may, there was an insurmountable obstacle to the application of the the Convention. The Convention does not lay down rules relating to acts that are committed not by the occupying troops, but by *other armed forces* that do not belong to the occupying army. Indeed, when article 29 defines the occupier's responsibility for the treatment of the inhabitants of the occupied territories ('protected persons'), it only speaks of crimes *committed directly* by the agents of the occupier, not of crimes perpetrated by other military forces. This point is, instead, dealt with in the First Additional Protocol of 1977, so often quoted by the MacBride Commission. However, the Protocol was never signed and still less ratified by Israel. Therefore, the latter is not bound by it (the few, casual remarks the Commission made to the effect that Israel ought to have respected it notwithstanding are very unconvincing).

It is thus apparent that although the Commission did indeed invoke international law, it did so unskilfully and erroneously, for reasons that are difficult to understand. Like the Kahan Commission, it also did considerable harm – though for different reasons – to the legal rules that govern the international community, not to mention the requirements of humanity and justice which they reflect.

The pronouncement of the UN General Assembly

Within the wider framework of debate on the Middle Eastern crisis, which drags on from year to year, in December 1982 the UN General Assembly briefly discussed the question of Sabra and Shatila. With a huge majority (123 votes in favour, no contrary vote and 22 abstentions) it approved a resolution in which first it mentions the Convention on Genocide of 9 December 1948 and the Fourth Geneva Convention of 1949; it goes on to state that it '*Condemns* in the strongest terms the largescale massacre of Palestinian civilians in the Sabra and Shatila refugee camps'; and '*resolves* that the massacre was an act of genocide'.[5]

At this point the jurist might rest content. At last an authoritative political organ had spoken for the consciences of all men, condemning the massacre in unequivocal terms based on a solemn legal act that the same Assembly had approved as far back as 1948. However, the satisfaction of jurists – and, I may add, of all those who believe in the importance of drafting and applying 'forward-looking' principles that reflect those humanitarian values that are so frequently trodden underfoot – is anything but complete. For although the General Assembly was right in not covering a serious collective crime under the cloak of silence, it went wrong on two points.

First, its resolution was not preceded either by a careful and thorough inquiry, or by an exhaustive debate on the facts and on the legal implications of labelling the massacre a genocide in the technical sense (the Cuban delegate, who introduced the draft resolution in the name of all its proponents, merely observed that it was 'self-explanatory'). The label was applied more for political considerations (or even for reasons of propaganda) than for humanitarian reasons. It was not the outcome of an unbiased reflection on what had occurred and on how to punish the guilty parties. To a large extent this explains why many states expressed reservations, either before or after the resolution was passed. Among these were Spain, Denmark (in the name of the ten EEC countries), Israel, the United States, Finland, Sweden, Turkey and Canada; to these we should add two Third World states: Singapore and the Philippines. Basically, what bothered these countries was the tendency of the General Assembly to use vague and imprecise language even in referring to very serious events and precise legal concepts that require extremely careful handling. But, above all, these countries noted that it was not one of the General Assembly's duties to describe the Sabra and Shatila massacres, or other similar acts, as acts of genocide as defined in the 1948 Convention.[6] Naturally, one can disagree with these criticisms (and I, for one, feel that to a certain extent they are untenable). But the fact remains that they voiced justifiable political and diplomatic chagrin, though worded in legal terms, in their dismay at the hurried manner in which the Assembly had delivered its verdict, a haste that was all the more worrying since the Assembly's resolution could be exploited as a dangerous precedent on other occasions when the facts were less macroscopic and dramatic than those of Sabra and Shatila.

Another grave flaw in the resolution is, in my opinion, even more disturbing, as it reveals an intention to use the resolution as a political instrument and a tool for propaganda. The General Assembly took no further steps after expressing its verbal condemnation, as if, by describing the Sabra and Shatila slaughter as 'genocide', it had obliterated all possible consequences of the crime. Instead, it should have taken the ulterior step of exhorting states to seek out and punish the perpetrators of that massacre. It could also have requested Israel to mete out the necessary punishment. I have already said that Israel proved its undoubted courage and moral uprightness in trying to punish the Israelis who were 'indirectly responsible'; but it did not seek out and try the *real perpetrators* of those crimes. The General Assembly could have exhorted Israel, as well as Lebanon and the other states involved, to pursue the Phalangist culprits and drag them before a court. Yet it confined itself to defining the act of 'genocide', as if the epithet alone were strong enough to render justice to the innocent victims. Once again the General Assembly revealed its impotence, on this occasion aggravated by the fact that international law possessed the necessary 'tools', that the Assembly either could not, or did not want to use.

What rules were applicable?

Rules did exist by which to judge the massacre in all its aspects and to reach a just 'decision'. Let me now take a quick look at these rules.

The slaughter in Sabra and Shatila took place during the military occupation of the area by Israel. It is quite true that the Israeli armed forces entered Lebanon not to fight the legal government of that country but, with the help of one of the warring factions (the Phalangists), to destroy the armed forces of another group (the Palestinians). However, it is impossible to call Israel's presence in Lebanon by any other name than the military occupation by one sovereign state of the territory of another sovereign state. Thus the applicable rules were those that govern armed conflict, especially the rules on the military occupation of territories belonging to other states.

Among the general rules governing armed conflict, one seems particularly appropriate for the 'episode' that we are examining: military *commanders* are responsible for crimes committed by the forces under their command (or at least under their 'control'), if they have done nothing to *prevent* or have not taken steps to *punish* these crimes. This rule is of fairly recent formation, crystallizing soon after the Second World War. Before that, military commanders were responsible only if they had *ordered* their subordinates to commit war crimes (the massacre of civilians, the maltreatment of prisoners, the destruction of historical monuments, etc.) However, the trial of a Japanese general in the late 1940s marked the turning point. Tomoyuki Yamashita had commanded the Japanese forces that occupied the Philippines from October 1944 to September 1945. After the defeat of Japan, he was accused by the Americans of not preventing his troops from committing crimes against citizens of the United States and their Allies (the killing of civilians and prisoners of war; sacking; the destruction of religious buildings). Yamashita was found guilty, first by a US Military Commission, and then by the Supreme Court of the United States to which he had appealed. He was sentenced to death and hanged by order of General Douglas MacArthur, the supreme commander of the Allied forces in Japan.[7] During the trial, it became quite clear that not only had Yamashita not ordered the crimes committed by his troops, but he had been kept entirely in the dark; besides, he could have done little to stop them, because the US armed forces were creating a state of maximum chaos with the deliberate intention of destroying the organization and authority of the Japanese army. Yamashita was sentenced even though he had infringed no specific rule, and no precedent existed; furthermore, two Supreme Court judges had expressed their dissent in very clear terms (in particular, judge Murphy used severe words to condemn, both from a legal and a military point of view, the decision of the US Military Commission and the majority decision of the Supreme Court). The judgement was obviously unjust: Yamashita was sentenced to death for something that was not forbidden at the time when it was committed. Nevertheless, the decision led to the formation of a new international rule: *ex injuria jus oritur*. Proof that the new rule has crystallized can be found in the fact that the military manuals of Great Britain (1958),[8] the United States (1956 and 1976)[9] and Israel (1963)[10] all confirm it in very clear terms, for they hold an officer responsible not only for committing or ordering a war crime, but also if he failed to prevent or punish it (a rule along these lines was also included in the First Additional Protocol of 1977, article 87).

The facts of Sabra and Shatila should have been examined in the light of that general rule. The Israeli military commanders wielded effective power over the Phalangist troops. It was their duty to prevent the massacre (the killing of civilians was both a war crime and genocide, because its intention was to exterminate an ethnic group as such). Once they knew the slaughter had started, the commanding officers were duty bound to prevent it going any further. It is quite immaterial that the Phalangist soldiers were not part of the Israeli troops. As I have just said, according to the international rule, what counted was that the Israeli army had the effective power to direct and control the Phalangist troops.

After the slaughter, it was Israel's duty to seek out and punish not only those directly responsible, but also the military commanders who had done nothing to avert or to stop it. The fact that Israel did nothing of the sort to *the Phalangists* who had perpetrated such heinous crimes could have been impugned – and this is the important point – by any state party to the 1948 Convention on Genocide (which binds numerous states, including Israel). Indeed, article 8 of the Convention allows each contracting state to request the 'competent organs' of the United Nations to adopt the measures foreseen in the UN Charter to prevent and repress acts of genocide. Thus, any of those states could have requested the General Assembly to discuss the massacre and solicit Israel to punish those directly responsible and submit the Israeli commanding officers who had not prevented or stopped the slaughter to a proper criminal trial. Alas, once again short-term political considerations were allowed to prevail over the most elementary requirements of justice.

Legal imperatives and political 'expediency'

Readers will now feel that what I have outlined so far only confirms, without a shadow of doubt, that international law is impotent, because it does not possess a secular arm by which to impose respect for its imperatives. In the words of Hobbes, 'covenants, without the sword, are of no strength to secure a man at all'.[11] I cannot agree. In this particular case, as in many others, the rules by which to assess the facts existed. Furthermore, there existed also international procedures for the application of these rules. If law kept silent and only a faint, deformed echo reached us via the decisions and opinions of the three bodies that examined the massacre, this is because political (or even partisan) considerations impeded or deflected the strict observance of the law. However, unlike other instances of wholesale slaughter, in this case the pressure of public opinion was kept up and the moral rectitude of the Israeli judges ensured that the ethical and religious aspects of the affair never disappeared from view and that the responsibility of some of the guilty parties (though only to a limited extent) was brought to light. The fact remains, however, that the full potential of international law was not exploited. Above all, an important occasion was lost to prove how certain legal rules distill humanitarian values and, where the political will exists, how these rules can affect relations between states as well as between states and individuals.

The light of justice remained hidden under a bushel. Once, few people outside Lebanon had heard of the Sabra and Shatila camps. Now they are notorious both for having been the scene of massacres and for having become hotbeds for young terrorists. Today, the names of the two camps must be added to the long list of hitherto unknown villages and towns that recall abhorrent misdeeds and make us all shudder with horror and shame: Auschwitz, Dachau, Oradour-sur-Glane, Katijn, Hiroshima, Nagasaki, Soweto, My Lai . . .

6

Crime without Punishment
The Captain Astiz affair

Law is a two-faced Janus

Problems, to which common sense and certain fundamental principles of logic and justice hold the key, are often locked away behind legal rules and institutions that prevent their solution. The 'man in the street' then seems entirely justified in venting his fury and contempt on the legal edifice, built of quibbling rules and irritating prohibitions. Yet, the issue is a more complex one than would appear at first glance. First, because law turns a 'deaf ear' to certain cases only when *other* (economic or political) interests are at stake and conflict with those presented in court. It is thus futile to inveigh against 'law' in the abstract, because the true 'culprits' are politicians, diplomats and others, who choose to ignore the rights and aspirations that are being set aside. As Salvatore Satta, the Sardinian jurist and novelist, wrote: 'life itself is cruel, and law perfectly reflects all the cruelty of life.'[1]

Second, 'law' never offers a clear-cut solution to a problem. We all know – none better than criminal lawyers – that law is by nature many-faceted; it never gives one, and only one, answer to the queries of mankind. Thus, when it looks as if the legal rules themselves stand in the way of the appropriate and logical solution, that solution does exist, so long as one is prepared to delve into case-law and legal norms. 'Men of law' who are not prepared to go to such lengths ignore the dictates of justice and rationality because they prefer to look no further than a traditional reading of the law.

Here I should like to clothe the bare bones of my argument in the flesh and blood of a recent case that is well worth pondering.

Captain Astiz's crimes

The Argentinian Captain Alfredo Astiz has become notorious, not because of his virtues or exceptional abilities, but for a precocious capacity for inflicting pain. During the dark years of Argentina's recent history, as a twenty-year-old officer in that country's navy, Astiz soon became known for his skill in making people 'disappear' and in torturing and killing defenceless citizens and foreigners. Among the latter were a seventeen-year-old Swedish girl (Dagmar Hagelin) and two French nuns (Alice Domon and Renée-Léonie Duquet), who 'disappeared' in 1977. As the head of a special naval squad, Astiz was accused by various Argentinian and international organizations of having commanded and taken part in the torture and killing of the three women, as well as of others. The governments of Sweden and France approached the Argentinian administration and asked for an explanation of these disappearances, without success; this was to be expected, since Astiz was merely a cog in a monstrous machinery, set in motion by the political and military leaders of the Argentinian republic at that time.[2]

Perhaps his crimes would not have gained such notoriety if he had not been sent, in April 1982, to command the troops on the tiny island of South Georgia (which Great Britain considers one of its possessions, together with the Falklands/Malvinas). A few days later, the British reoccupied the island and Astiz and his men were taken prisoner. The photograph of Astiz signing the act of surrender was broadcast all over the world and made his name better known than ever. The French and Swedish governments promptly asked the United Kingdom to allow them to question Astiz about the crimes of which he stood accused. Greatly embarrassed, the British government asked the advice of the International Committee of the Red Cross in Geneva, since Astiz was obviously a prisoner of war. It would appear that the Committee – the international guarantor for the application of the 1949 Geneva Conventions on war victims – suggested that, as a prisoner of war, Astiz could not be sued for crimes he had committed before the war started and totally unconnected with that war. Uncertain of what to do, and unwilling to return him with the other prisoners of war to Argentina, the British decided to send him back to the United

Kingdom. Here he was imprisoned for five days and questioned by an English policeman, in partial compliance with the French and Swedish requests. Astiz refused to answer the questions. Meanwhile, as a measure of dissuasion, the Argentinian authorities let it be known that three British journalists had been arrested in Argentina and accused of espionage; the Argentinians were prepared to exchange them for Astiz.

On 10 June 1982, the British decided to hand Astiz back to the Argentinians 'in line with its policy of gentlemanly treatment for all Argentinian prisoners', adding that Great Britain did not want to hold Astiz as a subject for exchange with the three journalists and that 'whatever the imperfections [sic] of Argentina's system of justice, Britain must be seen to uphold the letter of the law'.

Astiz went home and the three British journalists were set free on 28 June. A few days later, a group of mothers of the *desaparecidos* asked an Argentinian federal court to set up an inquiry into the Captain's role in the disappearance of twelve people, among these the three foreign women. As far as we know their request went unheeded. In 1982, before the fall of the dictatorship, Astiz hit the headlines once again when his request to be allowed to go to South Africa (a country where he had served in a diplomatic mission) was turned down because the South Africans refused to grant him a visa (in March 1983). Recently, after democracy had been restored in Argentina, the international press took a new interest in him: in May 1984 he was court-martialled for handing South Georgia back to the British without putting up any resistance. Various cases have been brought against him for torture, to no avail. He has been acquitted for lack of evidence in one trial. Besides, President Alfonsin's statute of limitations (passed at the end of 1986) has now put a full stop to all such cases against military officers. Having convicted five former members of Argentina's military junta, as well as five other officers, the government obviously feels that any further convictions would have a destabilizing effect on the armed forces. A further blow to justice was delivered by the law on 'due obedience to superior orders' passed on 5 June 1987. As a result of the new trends in the Argentinian legislation, Astiz was eventually acquitted in 1987 both by the 'Supreme Council of Armed Forces' and by the Federal Court of Appeal.

The British reaction

It is easy to infer from the facts I have outlined that Great Britain preferred to hand over Astiz and avoid any 'retaliation' against the three journalists, who might have been tried and condemned for espionage by the Argentinian courts. Yet the British government also averred it was respecting the 'letter of the law'. Was the government, under English law, forced to hand over Astiz or, if not, what could have been done to investigate the Captain's guilt in a democratic system that guarantees the accused a fair trial?

First let us take the Third Geneva Convention of 1949 on prisoners of war. This treaty does not prohibit a state from initiating criminal proceedings against a prisoner of war for crimes committed before the hostilities began and which are totally unconnected with the war (article 85 merely provides that 'Prisoners of war prosecuted under the laws of the Detaining Power for acts committed prior to capture shall retain, even if convicted, the benefits of the present Convention.') Besides, the International Committee of the Red Cross produced a *Commentary* which also admits of such a possibility.[3] However, current practice interprets this and other rules of the Convention to mean that prisoners can only be tried for crimes connected with the war. The reasons given are that the belligerents might, otherwise, take unfair advantage of the rule and use it as a pretext to sue prisoners of war for alleged crimes perpetrated before the war, but in reality to 'punish' them for participating in the hostilities. This might induce the enemy to 'retaliate' by doing likewise, thereby setting in motion a spiral of legal violence, to the detriment of prisoners of war.

However, Great Britain's legal motives for handing over Astiz were not based only on the Geneva Conventions. As an English jurist pointed out in a learned journal, the government probably reasoned as follows: admitting the Geneva Convention will allow us to sue Astiz or to have him sued by others; we face the alternative either of prosecuting him ourselves, or of extraditing him to France or Sweden. The second alternative is out of the question; under English law extradition is possible only when it has already been agreed in a treaty with the interested country; the treaties with Sweden and France allow for the extradition of the accused only if the crime has been committed on the territory of the requesting state (in this case France or Sweden), but Astiz committed his crimes in Argentina. The first alternative is also questionable, at least according to a traditional reading of English law. In Great Britain *foreigners* can be incriminated only if they have committed crimes in the United Kingdom, or against British citizens. Thus there were no grounds by which Astiz could be impleaded. Besides, the Captain had acted for one of the government's military agencies. Any case against him would get tangled in yet another legal obstacle in the shape of the 'act of state doctrine', which prevents British courts from holding foreign agencies personally responsible for acts performed in their official capacity.

Digging in search of a different solution

Should we rest content with this interpretation of English and international law? The answer, I feel, is no. Let me enumerate the reasons why I think so.

First, the letter of the Geneva Convention does not exclude trying prisoners of war for ordinary crimes committed before hostilities began. Naturally, this rule requires careful interpretation to prevent the sort of abuse I mentioned earlier. One way to avoid the pitfall of reciprocal 'retaliations' is to allow the courts to hear only those cases that involve exceptionally grave crimes: cases of theft, armed robbery or even the murder of a relation or of a fellow soldier should not be included; only crimes against humanity, such as genocide or torture, should be brought to court. The gravity of the crime and its offence against human dignity should alone justify prosecuting the criminal.

Was it then possible to circumvent the regulations that prevented British courts from hearing the Astiz case? It is my view that international law could have lent a hand. To put it in a nutshell, a general international rule exists that bans torture as a crime against humanity. Given the 'international' nature of the crime of torture (in that if offends not only the victim or his countrymen, but the whole of mankind, and hence concerns also states other than those directly involved), each and every nation can *legitimately* try individuals accused of torture (though is not obliged to do so). This holds true even when the crime was committed abroad and affected foreigners. In other words, the international rule makes jurisdiction for acts of torture *universal*. This international rule might have been invoked, within the limits I have mentioned, in the Astiz case by British courts (which are expected to apply general international law as the 'law of the land'). Admittedly, Great Britain is fairly insular when it comes to applying international rules since, where these conflict with English law, the latter 'must' prevail. But in the Astiz case there did not appear to be any conflict between the two bodies of law. If anything, the international rule *completes* or *supplements* English law, by broadening the scope of a British court's jurisdiction.[4]

As to the 'act of state' doctrine, it can be said that it hardly applied at all. To a person charged with a 'crime against humanity' the protective screen of state sovereignty is of no avail; the accused *stands alone* before his judges (whether national or foreign). He alone must answer for his misdeeds, without any chance of appealing for help to the state authorities for whom he unwisely acted. (In another essay of this book I shall emphasize how, when the accused acted on superior political or military orders, this does not relieve him of responsibility; it can only be used as a mitigating circumstance.)

A couple of 'precedents'

At this point a reader might observe that it is easy for a man sitting peacefully at his desk 'to judge and pontificate,' since he runs no personal risk; whereas those who act directly in the name of the state – politicians, diplomats, judges – have to grapple with thorny issues of every kind and act with great circumspection, reluctantly setting aside their 'humanitarian' instincts. Yet my own 'pronouncements' were not thought up in a vacuum; they are based on valid precedent. Let me just mention two cases that bear me out.

The first regards the Italian Supreme Military Tribunal's decision in the *Wagener* case in 1950. The case involved some German soldiers accused of having illegally shot ten Italians during the war as a 'reprisal' for killing one of their own men. The Tribunal quoted the Italian military penal code, which reflects general international law when it declares that enemy soldiers can be sued for war crimes, even when they acted in obedience to their own military regulations. The Tribunal declared:

> By embodying high ethical and humanitarian values, these [Italian] norms are not limited in their effect to a given country, but are universal. The international law of war contains the principle, commonly accepted by all nations [. . .], that any state can itself punish members of the enemy forces, who have fallen into its hands, when they have taken part in acts that violate the international rules of war. This is true in all cases where the *common conscience of civilized peoples is offended by the performance of certain barbarous and inhuman acts.* Solidarity among nations, which unites them in the hope of finding the best way to mitigate the horrors of war, has led them to lay down *rules that know no frontiers and punish criminals wherever they may be.*

After denying that the war crimes it was discussing should be regarded as political offences the Tribunal then added:

> [they] do not offend the political interests of a given state, nor the political rights of one of its citizens. These are crimes of *lèse humanité* and, as we have seen, they are subject to universal and not merely territorial norms. Consequently, by their legal object and special nature, these crimes are of an opposite and different nature to political offences. The latter only affect the state against which they were committed. The former *offend all civilized nations and must be sought out and repressed just as piracy, the white slave trade, the sale of minors and slavery must be sought out and repressed, wherever these crimes are committed.*

To be sure, the remarks I have quoted[5] do not refer to crimes such as those committed by Astiz, but to the more 'traditional' class of 'war crimes'. However, although the subject of these remarks is different, they are worth remembering here because they underscore the importance of the concept of *lèse humanité*, together with the fact that some crimes must be of concern to all nations, whatever the victim's nationality or the precise spot in which they were committed.

Let us now take a look at the *Eichmann* case, the more pertinent of the two. The notorious Nazi colonel was tried in Jerusalem in 1961, on the basis of an Israeli law passed in 1950. Among other objections, Eichmann's counsel suggested that the Act was contrary to international law because it allowed the court to punish foreign citizens (Eichmann was German) for crimes committed abroad (in Germany and in the territories occupied by the Nazis) against foreigners (naturally,

Eichmann's victims did not possess Israeli citizenship when he applied the 'final solution' to them). These objections were rejected, first by the District Court of Jerusalem and later by the Supreme Court of Israel. The latter observed that crimes against humanity (such as the acts of genocide committed by Eichmann) were of a 'universal' nature: they 'can undermine the foundations of the international community as a whole and impair its very stability'; consequently the interest in preventing and punishing them, 'especially when they are perpetrated on a very large scale, must necessarily go beyond the borders of the state to which the perpetrators belong and which demonstrated tolerance or encouragement of their outrages'.[6] It was on account of 'the universal character' of these crimes that the Supreme Court upheld the *universal nature of jurisdiction* over them and, on that basis, it tried and convicted Eichmann.

The *Eichmann* case was particularly relevant as a precedent because the Israeli legal system is modelled on the English one. It is true that the Israeli courts were able to base their decisions on a written law (the 1950 Act) that specifically conferred jurisdiction on them for crimes such as those of which Eichmann stood accused. However, the Supreme Court not only invoked that law but also added an important point. It specified that, had there been no such written law, Israeli courts would still have had jurisdiction because of the very nature of the crimes attributed to Eichmann: crimes that offend the feelings and dignity of mankind. As the Court said, 'it is the universal character of the crimes in question which vests in every state the authority to try and punish those who participate in their commission.'[7]

The same criterion could have been applied to the Astiz case: torture is now universally recognized as a crime against humanity. Besides, like many other states, Great Britain has long since supported within the United Nations the rule on universal jurisdiction which was then embodied in the 1984 UN Convention on torture.

The *Eichmann* case and the pronouncements of numerous states (including Great Britain) at the United Nations might have induced the British to see that justice was done, and try Astiz in Great Britain. No one could have objected that the British judges would have been prejudiced in their decisions by the fact that Astiz was an enemy. The mature and balanced character of British justice is well known. Besides, yet another factor would have ensured that the decision was rigorous and impartial: none of Astiz's victims had been a British subject.

Finally, had the British authorities desired to shun criminal proceedings against Astiz, they could have followed the example of their American counterparts in the *Filartiga* case (described in the last essay of this book) and initiated a civil suit against him, at the behest of the victims' laywers. To sue Astiz for damages for the victims of his tortures would have had the merit, as in the *Filartiga* and *Siderman* cases, of placing his crimes under a strong limelight, for all the world to see.

By way of conclusion

Once again the tug-of-war between the *requirements of justice* and the *self-serving interests of sovereign states* ended in victory for the latter. It is beyond question that the British government could not ignore the fate of the three journalists held by the Argentinians. But was there no other means for preventing Argentina from carrying out odious 'retaliations' had Astiz been made to answer for his crimes before a British court, or had he been made to pay compensation to his victims' relations? We must not forget that the Argentinians took *only one* prisoner of war, whereas Britain captured hundreds of enemy soldiers. By this I do not mean that the British could have retaliated against their prisoners of war – this is explicitly forbidden by the Third Geneva Convention of 1949. However, instead of treating the Argentinian POWs as well as it did, Great Britain could have applied the Convention to the letter. Indeed, Britain was not at the mercy of its enemy. Above all, had Argentina persisted in perpetrating grave violations, Britain could have applied sanctions against it.

This would have been a steep and arduous path to choose and it is easy to see how much more simple – for obvious 'reasons of state' – was the other course of handing over Astiz to his superiors. Is it just, however, that horrendous crimes, which so many people allege he committed, should go unpunished? In this case, law itself opened a convenient back door by which to evade a difficult political and diplomatic situation that might well have led to even greater friction between the two countries. However, we must not forget that the law could have provided the courts with other solutions, difficult to choose but far closer to the ethics of humanity.

7

Klaus Barbie
The exemplary life of an executioner

Barbie's life and career

The name of Klaus Barbie was well known even before his expulsion from Bolivia in 1983; his trial in France promised to be sensational and the media gave him plenty of coverage. A brief outline will, therefore, be sufficient to remind the reader of the main points in his career.

Barbie was born in 1913 in Bad Godesberg of a Catholic family from the Saarland, an area that borders on France, hence the rather un-German surname. He was five when the German Empire was defeated in 1918; his father had been wounded and captured at Verdun by the French and had later fought against them when they occupied the Ruhr Valley. Of modest means, the family was hard hit by the post-war economic crisis and lived for the day of Germany's revenge. It is hardly surprising that Barbie joined the Hitler-Jugend in 1933 and, two years later, at the age of twenty-two, took the decisive step of going into the SD (Sicherheitsdienst – the 'security police', a branch of the SS, set up to protect the Nazi party and uphold its ideology). Two years later, he became a member of the Nazi party itself. He immediately attracted the attention of his superiors in the SD for his boldness and his quick, rational mind. In 1940 he was made a sub-lieutenant in the SS and sent to newly invaded Holland. Here, in Amsterdam, he proved he could act with rapidity and determination, 'qualities' that were to the fore when, on two occasions in 1941, he had to deal with the Jewish community. In the first, two Jewish businessmen decided to put up some resistance to German harassment; Barbie had one condemned to death and executed and the other deported to a concentration camp, where he later died. In the second, the leaders of the Jewish community were seduced by Barbie's promises of help: as a result 300 young Jews were arrested and deported to Mauthausen. These and other exploits led to his promotion. Lieutenant Barbie was sent for a while to Gex, on the Swiss border in occupied France. Then, at the age of twenty-nine, he was transferred to Lyons, where he spent twenty-two months. This was the apex of his career; the rest of his life was spent in hiding, until 1983.

Lyons had been briefly occupied by German troops in June 1940. Then the *Wehrmacht* left and the city was taken over by the Vichy government. Lyons became the epicentre of the Resistance which, however, was weak and divided. There were three groups: Combat, Libération-Sud and the Franc-tireurs. Besides infighting between the groups, the Resistance lacked funds and arms. Only the communists were in full fighting form, but they did nothing at all until after Germany broke the non-aggression Pact and invaded the Soviet Union (21 June 1941). Only then did they become extremely effective saboteurs. From November 1942, when the Allies landed in North Africa, the Germans decided to take things in hand: they occupied Vichy France, using the Pétain government as a front, as well as the South of France ('operation Attila'). This brought about various changes, including the need to exercise greater control over the French. Barbie was sent to the *Einsatzkommando* of the SS in Lyons to head Section IV (the Gestapo or 'Secret Police'). His orders were to crush political crimes, fight against communism and sabotage, and carry out the Nazi policy for the Jewish community. On 17 February 1943, the Vichy regime passed the disgraceful decree on the *Service du Travail Obligatoire*, by which all Frenchmen who had come of age were required to go to Germany to work for the Third Reich. Thousands of young Frenchmen took to the woods and were enrolled in the ranks of the Maquis, thereby creating a new menace for the German occupying forces. Furthermore, in London, De Gaulle decided the Resistance needed bolstering up and sent Jean Moulin as his personal representative to France. The young *préfet* parachuted into France in January 1942. Within a year he had worked effectively to reunite the various groups and make the Resistance more efficient under De Gaulle's leadership.

Not a bit discouraged by this turn of events, Barbie applied his gifts of tenacity and perceptiveness to the new task. The idea of making arrests of great numbers in the Resistance movement and Jewish community obsessed him. His task was made easier by the partisans' mistakes and lack of organization; by the willingness of many French to collaborate, including a few Resistance fighters who turned coat after being tortured; by the co-operation of a few Jewish organizations, either too credulous or, occasionally, eager to collaborate; by the scant or non-existent support given to the Jews by the Christian population. Barbie was immensely successful. Jews and partisans were arrested and tortured by the hundreds, many died and the others were deported. His greatest triumph, however, the one that has made him notorious and will ensure that his name is removed from the cauldron of daily news to flow in the select river of history, was the arrest and murder of Jean Moulin.

In 1943 Jean Moulin was 45. His first acquaintance with the Germans had been in 1940, as the *préfet* of Chartres. At the time he refused to comply with a Nazi request to sign a declaration in which it was asserted (falsely) that some women and children (killed in a nearby village during a bombardment) had been massacred by the Senegalese troops of the French army. He was arrested and tortured; he then tried to kill himself by cutting his throat with the broken glass of a bottle, because he did not want to give in to Nazi bullying. He was saved and released by the Vichy government and given leave of absence from his post. After a couple of months he escaped to London, where he met De Gaulle. The general was so impressed by the young *préfet's* intelligence and far-sightedness he decided to send him as his representative to France. Though his political leanings were radical socialist and, therefore, not exactly in line with De Gaulle's, Jean Moulin accepted his new job with enthusiasm. He was in a turmoil of activity when Barbie arrested him in Lyons. The arrest interrupted a meeting of Resistance leaders he had called to discuss future precautions and strategy after the Gestapo had arrested General Charles Delestraint, the head of the Armée secrète in Paris. The meeting was a haphazard affair: no guards had been placed around the villa in Caluire (a Lyons suburb) where it was being held and other precautions were almost non-existent; even fate seemed to be against the partisans.[1] Led by Barbie, the Gestapo arrested all the leaders but one, René Hardy, who managed to escape and was later accused (both by his fellow partisans and by Barbie himself) of having betrayed his colleagues. Jean Moulin was tortured, then taken to the SS headquarters in Paris and, according to the Germans, died on a train bound for Berlin. The SS high command was furious with Barbie, who had 'managed' his famous victim without extracting a word of confession. Barbie replied that Jean Moulin had repeatedly tried to commit suicide: his death was the consequence of these attempts. Despite the criticism, Himmler promoted him to captain of the SS.

In August 1944, the tide turned and the SD had to leave Lyons, after destroying numerous documents and killing many collaborators, irrefutable proof of a dirty conscience. Barbie disappeared for a time. Then the *second period* of his life began, working for American intelligence.

After fleeing to Germany, Barbie was arrested, but managed to escape. At this point he was approached by the American Counter-Intelligence Corps in occupied Germany, which was looking for helpers in its fight against communism, both in the Eastern bloc, in other secret services and in the new French government, which it suspected of being heavily infiltrated. Barbie and the other Nazi agents had a wide network of informers that proved extremely useful to the CIC. Barbie continued to help them for three years (1947–50) and, in exchange, was protected by the Americans from the French police, who were conducting inquiries into Jean Moulin's murder. The French were allowed to question Barbie in 1948 and at the beginning of 1949, but only on a limited number of issues and only in the presence of Americans. When the second trial of René Hardy started in France, so many obstacles were created to Barbie's being even a *witness* (no question here of *prosecuting* the Nazi officer) that the French gave up the attempt. In September 1948, the inquiring magistrate of the Paris military court told his colleague in Lyons that, for 'reasons of the national security of the United States, the Americans have said that K. Barbie cannot be handed over to the French'.[2]

However, pressure from French public opinion was such that the Americans decided to stop using Barbie for their own ends. It is even suggested, in one of Barbie's biographies, that they thought seriously of getting rid of him once and for all.[3] In any case, he was 'sacked' on 19 January 1951 and allowed to depart for Bolivia, thanks to the 'good offices' of various organizations, including the Red Cross (which, presumably, knew nothing of his past).

Here begins the *third chapter* of Barbie's life. He spent 32 years in Bolivia, mostly in hiding, helped by the complicity of the authorities there. Not that this was a period of reflection and expiation! He never seems to have recanted his Nazi ideology. Indeed, at a party given by the ambassador of the Federal Republic of Germany in La Paz for the German community there, he took leave of his host with a 'Heil Hitler!' The ambassador had him thrown out of the embassy and he yelled back that the Nazis would repay the diplomat in kind as soon as he returned to Germany.

In 1983 the wind finally shifted. A democratic President, Herman Siles Suazo, was elected in Bolivia. Besides, there had been a left-wing government in France since 1981, with many ex-resistance fighters among its members (Mitterrand, Mauroy, Cheysson, Hernu); Robert Badinter, the Minister of Justice, was the son of a Jew deported to the Sobibor concentration camp, from which he never returned. Furthermore, one of the Elysée advisers, Régis Debray, had fought in Bolivia side by side with Che Guevara; he was imprisoned there and, on being released, had helped Mr and Mrs Klarsfeld in their attempt to kidnap Barbie in 1972–3. On 5 February, Barbie was expelled from Bolivia for having given a false name when he was naturalized (in 1957); the French had him arrested in French Guyana and flown to Lyons. For symbolical reasons, he was then imprisoned for a few days in Montluc gaol, where he had interrogated and tortured so many partisans and Jews. So begins the *fourth chapter* of his life, with a predictable ending. Barbie is now 75; it is unlikely he will ever leave prison, where tardy retribution has caught up with him, but seems to have left him unrepentant.[4]

Why did Barbie commit his crimes?

Of the numerous queries raised by the Barbie affair, I shall examine only three. First, why did the French decide to prosecute him again after a lapse of so many years? Then, were the Lyons judges right in drawing a distinction between war crimes and crimes against humanity? Finally, why has such a well-known leftist lawyer as Jacques Vergès decided to fight furiously to defend a man at the other extreme of the ideological spectrum?

Before answering these questions, I would like to deal with a more general issue, which concerns us all: why in this world 'of sound and fury' did some men like Barbie fling themselves so ferociously upon their fellow men? I don't mean this to be a general metaphysical inquiry into the origins of evil. I am interested in the here and now: why did a young man, who grew up within the Western democratic system between two world wars, commit crimes that should be repugnant to any civilized human being?

Some of Barbie's biographers have placed the spectacles of psychoanalysis upon their noses to examine his childhood frustrations, his father's bitterness against the French, his tawdry petit bourgeois life in a family disrupted by war and poverty. But the results are somewhat tentative, since they are based on very flimsy material. (Unlike Freud, in his study of President Schreber, they had no diary on which to base their analyses.) Others have insisted on historical fact: the post-war economic crisis in Germany; Hitler's accession to power, which could be explained by various circumstances, including the anti-semitism rife in German society. All this helps to throw some light on Barbie's behaviour. The racist ideology of the Third Reich and the creation of an efficient but pitiless totalitarian machine were the necessary premises to his barbaric ferocity. Besides, he was acting in an *emergency*: a war was on and it was his job to repress all individuals who threatened (the partisans) or could contaminate (the Jews) the system of *law and order* he represented. This was certainly not the first time that men had behaved ruthlessly towards their 'enemies', that is those who 'are not one of us' and whose 'religion is not ours'. The words 'the fire of rebellion can only be put out by the freezing wind of terror or by torrents of blood' were written in the seventeenth century by a man of God, Cardinal Sforza Pallavicino, in a history in defence of the Council of Trent, written for the Curia.[5] I doubt Barbie knew the quotation, but he did follow the advice day by day in Lyons, making it the insignia of his life there.

Can it be said that Barbie was merely applying Nazi policy and carrying out his orders to the letter? I do not agree that the savagery with which he tortured, maimed and murdered his enemies can be explained in purely sociological or historical terms. Neither of these sciences seems able to pierce the murky twilight surrounding such incomprehensible actions. Historians themselves (for example Bullock, Schramm and Bracher) have concluded that Nazi anti-semitism is an inexplicable phenomenon. One of the most perceptive witnesses to the horrors of the Final Solution, Primo Levi, who described life at Auschwitz in *Se questo è un uomo* (If this be a man), has written that 'no one can understand what happened, indeed no one *should* understand, because to understand is to justify.'[6] Perhaps to a certain extent this dark area of the psyche coincides with our 'free will', an area beyond the effects of psychological, economic or historical conditioning where decisions are made for which we must answer as *individuals* because they are *ours alone*, even though when we take them we are part of the social fabric.

This dark area is admittedly a barrier to our attempts to grasp reality with its myriad ramifications. On the other hand, that same area allows us to insist that the perpetrators of heinous crimes are brought to justice. How could we expect to try and condemn the criminal, if his actions were merely the result of a determination extraneous to him?

Why try Barbie so long after the event?

It has been observed that Barbie was a finished man even before he was expelled from Bolivia. First there had been the death of his son in a hang-glider accident, then that of his wife. He was old, unwell and alone. His life was nearing the end of its cycle when he was picked up by the French and flown to Lyons to spend his last years in prison before, during and after his trial. What made the French decide to drag him to court, almost forty years after he had committed the crimes of which he stood accused and for which he had already been twice condemned to death by default? A 'thirst for justice' or 'revenge' are the most obvious answers, but also, perhaps, those furthest from the truth. Besides, it would certainly be presumptuous, as well as impossible, to see into the minds and hearts of members of the French administration. It is safer to limit our ruminations to a few cautious conjectures on what made the state, that 'cold monster', tick in this case.

Before we begin, it is worth wondering what induced the victors to hold trials against the Germans and their collaborators after the Second World War, and what, more recently, has persuaded governments to hold similar trials for war crimes and crimes against humanity. The answer may help us to formulate our conjectures on the Barbie case.

By 1942 the Allies knew the Nazis were committing atrocities and had begun to wonder how to react and how to punish those responsible. After the defeat of Germany, the British stated that it was enough to arrest and hang those primarily responsible for determining and applying Nazi policy, without wasting time on legal procedures; minor criminals, they suggested, could be tried by specially created tribunals.[7] However, neither Harry Truman nor Henry Stimson, the US Defense Secretary, agreed; nor, indeed, did Stalin. In the end, they prevailed, and the International Military Tribunal was set up in Nuremberg to try the 'great Nazi criminals', while lesser Allied tribunals in the four occupied zones of Germany were to deal with minor criminals. The Americans advanced three arguments to support their view, later accepted by the other Allies. First, how could a defeated enemy be condemned without due process of law? To hang them without trial was do away with one of the mainstays of democracy: no one can be considered guilty until his crimes have been proved in a fair trial. To relinquish such a fundamental principle would have put the Allies on a par with the Nazis who had galloped roughshod over so many principles of justice and of civilization itself, when they had held mock trials, or punished those allegedly guilty without even taking them to court. The Nuremberg trial was to uphold the *postulates of justice*.

Second, the crimes committed by the Third Reich and its Nazi officials were so appalling that some visible record had to be left for posterity. A trial held on a grand scale would allow the Tribunal to gather a huge pile of records useful not only in court, but to historians and to the generations to come. The trial would help to *build an archive of historical documents that might otherwise vanish*; it would also *serve as a lesson in history for future generations*.

Third, those who set up the Nuremberg Tribunal felt that the dramatic rehearsal of Nazi crimes – and of racism and totalitarianism – would make a deep impression on world opinion. The faces of the Nazi chiefs had to become household property throughout the world via films and photographs in the press. All those who had fought against the Axis powers, or had suffered invasion, had to know exactly what these great criminals looked like, how they reacted to the accusations, to questioning and to what the witnesses testified. This was the only way to combat the myth of the Nazi state, that massive, anonymous machine that had loured menacingly over everyone for so long. The trial was to *render great historical phenomena plainly visible.*[8]

Let us now ask what lay behind two other famous trials, that of Eichmann and that of Lieutenant Calley. Why did the Israelis decide to try Eichmann themselves, rather than subject him to an international tribunal (as Karl Jaspers and Nathan Goldmann, the chairman of the World Jewish Congress, had suggested)?[9] Probably, David Ben Gurion's main reason for insisting that the trial be held in Israel and that all of the judges be Israelis was to *legitimize the birth of the state of Israel.* The dramatic evocation of the 'holocaust' justified and underscored the need to create a Jewish state. Besides, in giving a fair trial to a man who had been responsible for the deaths of millions of Jews, it proved how mature and impartial was the judiciary of that state.

The Calley case is rather different. The lieutenant was accused of crimes committed in Vietnam, not during the Second World War. Furthermore, the trial was held by the very state of which Calley was a citizen: an extraordinary event. It was to be a lesson for present and future generations. Why did the American army have him court-martialled? Events before and after the trial indicate quite clearly that the US government decided something had to be done to placate the horror public opinion felt, at home and abroad, at the My Lai incident. The trial was proof of respect for the great principles of American justice; it was held under the eagle eye of a highly critical public, sick to death of the Vietnam war. In fact, the trial was virtually *ordered by the law and by public opinion.* Subsequent reductions in his sentence during the legal proceedings and President Nixon's pardon prove that the Calley trial was the price paid to formal democracy. However, 'realism' later got the upper hand and Calley was allowed to go free.[10]

To return to the Barbie case, various reasons have been aired in France as to why he was to be tried again. Some writers remarked that the newly formed Socialist government was having its first reversals in 1983: it needed extra prestige and the whole-hearted support of the population, which was drifting away.[11]

Others, ignoring possible political motives, have emphasized what they feel *ought* to be the main reason for the trial. On 7 February 1983, Raymond Aron wrote in *L'Express*[12] that the trial offered an occasion to condemn the essence of Nazism: 'an ideology that led inexorably to crimes against humanity, since it ostracized certain ethnic groups as such'. This well-known political theorist felt the opportunity should not be lost to try to condemn both Nazi ideology and all other totalitarian ideologies, whether of the left or the right. On the other hand, Jean Jacques Bloch, the chairman of the Jewish Council for the Rhône-Alpes region, and Marc Aron, chairman of CRIF (Conseil représentatif des institutions juives de France) in Lyons, both agreed that the trial was to teach the young the extremes to which Nazi anti-semitic policy led.[13] Finally, Jean Julliard echoed these ideas in the *Nouvel Observateur*. He added that the court case was to pour shame on all those who had recently denied there had ever been a holocaust; it was also designed to debunk the idea of the 'collective heroism' of the French Resistance.[14]

All these writers, and all those who were of similar opinion, felt the trial *ought to transcend Barbie, the man*. As in the Nuremberg and Eichmann trials, the accused had a walk-on role to play in a drama of far wider scope; Barbie was really *a pretext to put the history of a people and of a nation in the dock*; an opportunity to exorcize far more disturbing ghosts.

Yet others think the real reason for having Barbie expelled, arrested and tried was the desire to avenge one of the greatest heroes of the French Resistance: Jean Moulin. This is the view of the French lawyer, Serge Klarsfeld,[15] one of the most persistent blood-hounds on the tracks of ex-Nazis. Some people even suggest[16] that to try Barbie for his crimes against humanity (which do not fall under the statute of limitations) and not for his war crimes (including the murder of Jean

Moulin), because under French law they are no longer punishable, served the interests of the government. No one needed to discover how many French men and women collaborated with the Germans, or which members of the Resistance betrayed their fellows. *Barbie would thus be punished for the murder of Jean Moulin, without opening old sores in France.*

If this last suggestion had been exact, the French would not have used Barbie as a pretext to examine events of a far wider scope, but would have vented on him alone the fury of their indignation for having tortured and killed the greatest leader of the Resistance. *No longer a mere puppet, he would have become the main target of French justice.*

The trial itself and its effects on French public opinion have, however, shown that the Barbie case was used both for its emblematic message, and to do justice – that is, to punish a man for crimes which were of a very serious nature, although committed more than 40 years ago.

War crimes and crimes against humanity

Barbie was tried for crimes against humanity. The Lyons judges pointed out that he had been prosecuted for his war crimes in 1952 and 1954 and had been condemned to death on both occasions. Under French law crimes can no longer be tried after 20 years; thus Barbie's previous sentences were automatically cancelled in 1972 and 1974 respectively. However, on 26 December 1964, the French government passed a law by which crimes against humanity do not fall under the statute of limitations. In fact, Barbie was tried for such crimes as concern the persecution of Jews, as well as that of some Resistance fighters who were also Jewish.

What is the difference between the two classes of crimes and were the Lyons judges right to draw the distinction? *War crimes* have long been recognized by international law and were finally crystallized at the end of the last century; their scope was further widened during the twentieth century. The category includes all serious violations – against both the *armed forces* and the *population of the enemy* – of the laws governing the conduct of hostilities. It also aims to protect all persons not directly involved in those hostilities. For example, it is a crime to torture or kill civilians or prisoners of war; to bomb undefended towns or churches and historical monuments; to use forbidden weapons. These crimes are punished so that the violence unleashed by war does not spill over beyond the limits set by international law. Traditionally, war criminals are punished either by their state of origin (as in the Calley case), or by its adversary (for obvious reasons the most common occurrence), or by an international tribunal (as in the Nuremberg and Tokyo trials after the Second World War). Usually, only those states directly involved in the war will prosecute for war crimes; *third* States normally do not show any interest in punishing the authors of such crimes, because they do not want to be involved either in an ongoing war or in one that has just ended. I should add that often, once the war is over, unless the victor wishes to exercise jurisdiction for war crimes committed by the enemy, the common practice is to wipe the slate clean, to help peaceful relations start anew.

During the Second World War it became apparent that the atrocities of the Nazis often fell outside the sphere of war crimes. One of the first to draw attention to the *inadequacy* of traditional law was a perceptive American jurist, Lieutenant Colonel Murray C. Bernays, then head of the Special Projects Office of the Defense Department. In 1944 Henry Stimson had asked for a memorandum on how to punish Nazi criminals once the war was over. In September, Bernays handed his superiors a vital document, which was to be the blueprint for Nuremberg and other minor trials.[17] He pointed out how numerous crimes committed by the Nazis (the persecution of German citizens for reasons of race, religion or politics) could not be classified as war crimes because they had either been performed before the war, or because the victims were not members of the *enemy* population, but Germans (and therefore subject only to German law). Besides crimes by Germans against other Germans, there were those committed against the citizens of states that were not under German occupation, such as Austrian Jews (Austria had never been occupied, but merely annexed), or people in certain areas of Czechoslovakia (in 1938–9). Bernays remarked, in the memorandum, that 'to let these brutalities go unpunished will leave millions of persons frustrated and disillusioned.' He added that the United States and the United Kingdom were already under pressure from various Jewish organizations to see that all such atrocities, and not only those against Jews themselves, should be punished.

The upshot was that by 1945 the Allies had decided to create a *new category of crimes*, moulded on Bernay's suggestions and on those of many others.[18] This was embodied in the London Agreement of 8 August 1945 (drafted jointly by the British, the Americans, the Russians and the French). To the category of war crimes were added two others: crimes against peace and crimes against humanity. Article 6, in which they are spelt out,[19] is thus one of the high points of legal civilization, even though this was only made possible by knocking down one of the fundamental principles of law: that no one should be punished for an act that was not considered criminal when it was performed (*nullum crimen sine lege*). Article 6 sets out to punish those who committed crimes against peace or against humanity even when, according to their own municipal law and to international law, such actions were still *legal*. How very unjust, some might object! This point was dealt with by another American who was to play an important role in Nuremberg, Colonel T. Taylor. In a memorandum for R. H. Jackson (whom President Truman had appointed chief of counsel for the prosecution of Axis criminality) he wrote:

> We need not shy off because of *ex post facto*. No one will be shocked by the doctrine that people who direct or do inhuman and barbarous things in the course of losing a war will be punished. Many would be shocked by the conclusion that such people may go scot-free unless a pre-existent law or rule can be cited.[20]

However, he added that when such a law or rule did exist it ought to be applied in preference to the two new categories.

The same argument – based on the idea that the moral precept *nullum crimen sine lege* must be 'set aside' when it would be palpably immoral to leave heinous crimes unpunished – was put forward by the International Tribunal in Nuremberg, though in this case it was referring principally to crimes against peace.[21]

Article 6, therefore, stands high as a bulwark against barbarity. Like most law, a cursory reading reveals the article to be only an arid, abstract and impersonal set of rules. Yet it is the offspring of the great suffering and humiliation of millions of people. It embodies their revolt against such inhuman treatment. It carries the solemn promise that such acts shall not be repeated. Article 6 is a mirror, reflecting the horrors of Auschwitz, Mauthausen, Ravensbrück, Treblinka and also Marzabotto and Oradour-sur-Glane. For the first time in the history of legal ethics an *international* set of rules was created to prohibit what had only been banned by municipal law (and not in all legal systems either: the laws of the Third Reich and, to some extent, of Fascist Italy are cases in point).

Let us take a moment to examine Article 6 *c* which deals with crimes against humanity. This is a sweeping ban, intended to form a rigid mesh with no loopholes through which the authors of horrific crimes may escape. All atrocities that do not come within the compass of war crimes are automatically covered by 'crimes against humanity'. The latter include two groups: 'murder, extermination, enslavement, deportation, and *other inhuman acts* committed *against any civilian population*'; and also '*persecution* on political, racial or religious grounds'. For instance, if the massacre of a civilian population, and the torture or deportation of a civilian (whether or not a partisan), cannot be punished as 'war crimes' – either because the population or the civilian were not in occupied territory, or did not belong to that country – the crime falls under those against humanity (if it is in some way connected to the war). The same goes for racial, political or religious persecution (again so long as it is connected to the war).

Since article 6 *c* was intended as a sweeping ban, the same act can be both a war crime and a crime against humanity. Thus the *torture* or *deportation* of a partisan (whether French, Yugoslav or Polish) are punishable under both sections. Similarly, 'murder, extermination, enslavement, deportation, and other inhuman acts' (including torture) committed against a civilian or a civilian population in occupied territory are war crimes, but also *crimes against humanity*. All such atrocious crimes *against the enemy* transcend the category of war crimes (that is crimes that only concern the belligerents) because they are the business of all civilized peoples, in as much as they offend human dignity, or our *condition humaine*.

In the Nuremberg trial this *double classification* was of little consequence, because almost all those accused of crimes against humanity were also accused of committing war crimes.

The Tribunal tended to regard the latter as inclusive of the former.

This distinction, set forth in general terms at Nuremberg without raising any practical problems, becomes extremely relevant in the Barbie case. Since his war crimes could not now be punished under French law, he could only be prosecuted for crimes against humanity. Which, then, of his many misdeeds were to be considered crimes against humanity and could lead to his conviction?

The inquiring magistrate, C. Riss, decided that all his crimes against members of the Resistance were war crimes. In his view Barbie was answerable only for crimes against the Jews who did not work in the Resistance.

The Chambre d'Accusation of Lyons agreed with his analysis; but various organizations of ex-deportees and ex-Resistance members, and even some associations for the defence of human rights, protested to the French Court of Cassation, arguing that the distinction was groundless. Both the Conseiller Rapporteur, Le Gunehec, and the Advocate General, Dontenville, upheld their view to a large extent, as did the Court itself. The main point made by the Cour de Cassation, and later reiterated by the Chambre d'Accusation of Paris, was that Barbie could also be tried for inhuman acts against members of the Resistance who were Jewish (such as Professor Marcel Gompel, a member of the Collège de France and a partisan in the Combat group, who was arrested and tortured to death by Barbie in Montluc prison), as well as for the deportation of Jewish partisans (like Régine Skorka-Jacubert, who was sent to a concentration camp), and finally for the torture and deportation of about 30 people from 1943 to 1944 for alleged activities in the Resistance and the deportation of partisans (600 members of the Resistance were sent to Germany on 11 August 1944 on the last convoy to a concentration camp before the liberation of France).

These important rulings of the Chambre d'Accusation of the Paris Court of Appeal[22] (to which the Cour de Cassation had transmitted the case) were based on the definition of crimes against humanity advanced by the Cour de Cassation, which observed that under article 6 *c* of the London Agreement crimes against humanity include, even when they are also war crimes as laid down in article 6*b*, all *inhuman acts* and *persecutions* that, in the name of a state pursuing a policy of ideological hegemony, were committed systematically, not only against people because they belonged to a racial or religious group, but also against people who oppose that policy, whatever form that opposition may take.[23]

This definition redressed the scales of justice after the formalistic interpretation given by judge Riss and Lyons Chambre d'Accusation had altered their equilibrium. On what arguments is it based? This the Cour de Cassation does not say. However, the reasons set forth by M. Le Gunehec when he summed up his presentation of the case were as follows:

If it can be said that there is a hierarchy of horror and cruelty, then crimes against humanity stand high above war crimes, because they not only violate the laws and customs of warfare laid down by men to salve their consciences and 'legitimize such use of force as is absolutely necessary'; above all these crimes offend the fundamental rights of mankind; the right to equality, without distinctions of race, colour or nationality, and the right to hold one's own political and religious opinions. Such crimes not only inflict wounds or death, but are aggravated by the voluntary, deliberate and gratuitous violation of the dignity of all men and women: these are victimised only because they belong to a group other than that of their persecutors, or do not accept their dominion.[24]

Here is a definition of crimes against humanity that is both acceptable and effective, so long as we take it in its broader meaning. In other words, it must be interpreted as also covering *inhuman acts* directed against *enemy civilians* not because they are Jewish, partisans or political opponents but *only* because they belong to the enemy. In any case, it was essential that M. Le Gunehec and the Paris Chambre d'Accusation should reject the restrictive interpretation of the Lyons judges.

Anyone who passionately desires to protect the fundamental values of all people must feel relieved that the Supreme Court of France, albeit after long and complicated vicissitudes, should have made a ruling that will serve to guide the decisions of other courts in the future. This, I hope, will help to judge not only crimes committed during the Second World War, but also crimes committed anywhere in the world which remain unpunished because governments are guilty of inertia, or because we ourselves, as the citizens of democratic states, often look on in silence.

A deeply disturbing character: Jacques Vergès

Complex and chequered as it already was, the Barbie affair was made murkier by the arrival on the scene of a famous lawyer: Jacques Vergès. He offered his services to Barbie a few months after the ex-Nazi was imprisoned, taking over from Alain de la Servette, who had been asked to take on Barbie's defence as the *batonnier* of the Lyons barristers. Who is Vergès and why did he decide to defend Barbie?

At the age of seventeen he took part in the liberation as a member of the Free French Army. In 1945 he joined the French Communist Party and became a leader in the youth movement. There he met another young leader, the Cambodian Pol Pot, who became a close friend and with whom he shared a hatred of colonialism. In 1954 he became a barrister and undertook the passionate defence of numerous Algerians, who had been tortured by the French. He married one of his clients, Djamila Bouhired, who had been tortured and sentenced to death in 1957 for having placed a bomb in the Algiers Milkbar. In 1957 he left the French Communist Party and began to defend Palestinians fighting against Israel; but in 1968 and 1969 the Israelis prevented him from defending two Palestinian commandos accused of acts of terrorism in Israel. In 1971 he disappeared, for almost nine years, and only reappeared in 1979. The mystery surrounding this period has only added to the fantastic tales told both by his enemies and his admirers. He then becomes even more closely associated with the defence of Palestinians and other alleged terrorists: Karl Croissant, the lawyer defending the Baader-Meinhoff group arrested by the French; the associates of the notorious Carlos; some members of Action Directe, the French left-wing group of terrorists; finally, some Palestinians accused of terrorism, including Georges Ibrahim Abdallah. When he took over Barbie's defence (his client claims never to have paid him a sou), public opinion was aghast: how could an ex-member of the Free French Army, who for years had pleaded the innocence of left-wing activists accused of terrorism, now assume the defence of a Nazi torturer?[25]

Several answers have been advanced to this query. Some dismiss Vergès as a megalomaniac and *agent provocateur*, who cynically uses the most notorious cases so as to be continually in the limelight. Others look to his political ideas for an explanation. He might have taken on the Barbie case because of his hate for colonialism and neo-colonialism, or possibly even for reasons of anti-semitism, which made him pounce on a case where he had to defend a man who had persecuted the Jewish community.

However, perhaps the most plausible explanation is based on Vergès's own ideas. In 1968 he published a lively, if rather chaotic, little book called *De la stratégie judiciaire*.[26] Here, as well as in numerous statements to the press and on television, he compared two opposite types of trials: 'trial of connivance' and 'trials of disruption' (*procès de rupture*). In the former the established order is respected, whatever the position of the accused, that is whether he declares his innocence or his guilt. Both the victim and the defendant belong to the same world as the judges, respect the same moral principles and would not dream of questioning the rules set by the establishment. In the latter case of a 'trial of disruption', the accused, though 'in chains, stands for a different order and for another world'.[27] His conception of what is lawful differs radically from that of his judges. It is his intention to attack the establishment in the name of a different legal order. For this reason, his main aim as a defence lawyer 'is not so much to get the defendant acquitted, as to highlight his ideas.'[28] In this kind of trial 'the personality of the man in the dock is left to one side; the debate is purely political, marked by brutal intransigence.'[29] Typical examples of suits such as these are the trial of Louis XVI by the French revolutionaires; that of Dimitrov, accused in 1933 before a German court of having set fire to the Reichstag; the 1953 trial in Cuba of Fidel Castro, after the failure of the revolt against the Batista regime; the various trials of Algerian FLN fighters in French courts. According to Vergès, the Dreyfus affair is a particularly vivid example of this difference. At first, Dreyfus and his lawyers saw it as a 'trial of connivance', in which every possible effort was made to prove that the defendant was not guilty because there was no compelling evidence that he had committed the crime. After Dreyfus had been condemned, Zola's *J'accuse* turned the trial topsy-turvy. The novelist made a virulent attack on the military hierarchy, accusing the French army of anti-semitism. 'The value of Zola's approach was to have been so bold as to abandon the terrain of law as such, to relinquish defence in favour of attack and the court room for the streets.'[30] 'Zola had a gift for exaggeration (*démesure*), without which no great disruptive defence is possible.'[31] He deserves the credit for fighting 'the classic form of judicial repression with the weapons of a politico-judicial war.'[32]

Herein lies the 'theoretical' key to the way Vergès conducted the suit: he considered the Barbie affair yet another 'trial of disruption'. Yet what specific aims did he pursue in this case? Here again his statements to the media can be useful.

Vergès has repeatedly reminded the French authorities that, after liberating France and punishing both collaborators and Nazi torturers, the French themselves were guilty of grave misdeeds in Algeria, between 1950 and 1960. They could not have a clear conscience. For Vergès, the Barbie trial was an opportunity to accuse the French establishment of committing similar atrocities in Algeria to those of the Nazis in occupied France and, furthermore, of wiping away the guilt of the French torturers with the amnesty laws of 1962 and 1968. He was also hitting out at the desire of numerous French families to forget that so many of their own relatives had collaborated with the Germans. As he said in September 1983, 'the Barbie trial is a mirror that will reflect all the ambiguities of the occupation.'[33]

This may be the interpretation that comes closest to the truth. However, much ambiguity also surrounds the lawyer himself; not least the fact that, in the Barbie case, his fees were allegedly to be paid by the Swiss protector of not a few Nazis, François Genoud, together with his obvious intention of provoking and mortifying the French. Was he justified in insisting that so many men and women examine their consciences, and if so, could he not have done so in a less theatrical way? Most disturbing of all is the poisonous anti-semitism that seems to flow into many of his flamboyant actions.

To sum up

Let me conclude this essay by answering three questions. In what way is Klaus Barbie different from so many other Nazi murderers? What lesson can be drawn from a perusal of his life? What should be done by people who still believe in Kant's maxim that man must always be considered an end and never a means – in other words by all those who firmly believe in the dignity of the human being? What can such people do to ensure that crimes committed long ago receive their just retribution; and how can they raise a dyke against the horrible misdeeds of our own times, wherever they are committed?

The first question is the easiest. Klaus Barbie would be indistinguishable from other Nazi bureaucrat-murderers of the Third Reich had Jean Moulin not been among his victims. His arrest, torture and killing transformed Barbie into a figure of Greek tragedy. All the tragic elements are there: the devious traitor; the implacable gaoler; the hero's refusal to betray his friends, despite his slow torture and death; fate, in the guise of a string of peculiar coincidences that made the hero's capture and murder possible. As Hannah Arendt said of Eichmann, there was no demon quality in Barbie. He was never an Iago, or even a Macbeth; just a diligent official who carried out the 'administrative massacres' that had been planned by the Nazi leaders.[34] Yet, unlike Eichmann, Barbie did not merely have thousands of more or less unknown men and women deported to their deaths. It was his sinister privilege to vent his destructive skills on the body of an exceptional man. Jean Moulin is one of the mythical heroes of modern France, and one of the most emblematic and enthralling figures of the post-war period. Barbie, and the collaborators and traitors who helped him, will endure as the shadow of that myth.

If his association with Jean Moulin has thrown him into the limelight of history, one must not forget that Barbie was also one of the 'officials supervising extermination'. He alone accounted for the deaths of thousands of men, women and children, whose names live on in the hearts of relations and friends and are inscribed on the memorials in villages and towns which saw them go to their deaths. As such he belongs to the history of Nazi villainy.

What lesson, then, can be learnt from Barbie's life and misdeeds? Leaving aside the historical and social milieu in which he grew up, it can be said that he was typical of those men Benedetto Croce called 'economico-juridical souls': people who possess no political ideal or ethical sense by which to temper the pressures of the prevailing 'ideology'; people who pursue purely selfish ends and who, therefore, fit into any public administration, whether totalitarian or democratic, whose orders they obey acritically and carry out with alacrity. In a society that offers 'economico-juridical souls' little scope, an oppressive establishment would be working on stony, infertile ground and there would be little room for those who despise their fellows.

Finally, let me answer the third question. The reason for asking such a question is due, though only in part, to the provocative attitudes and criticism of Jacques Vergès. What can a man, who refuses to be a passive spectator, do about serious crime and compromise in the *past*, and about the grave misdeeds committed *today* throughout the world? Although my answer is based on the Barbie affair, it can, perhaps, be applied to other circumstances as well.

I am among the first to admit that sovereign states – those 'mortal Gods' as Hobbes called them – have a logic all their own and often do not, or cannot, act with respect for the highest values of humanity. However, as to France, the very government Vergès accuses so virulently has recently adopted measures that are an attempt to put an end to past errors and indeed has helped the Court reach a just decision on Nazi acts of inhumanity and on French collaboration. As I have already discussed these measures, I shall merely enumerate them here. In 1966 a law was passed by which crimes against humanity could never become statute barred; in 1983, Barbie was arrested and imprisoned to await trial; the same year, parliament passed a new law allowing private organizations, set up to expose war crimes and crimes against humanity, to file suits for damages within the ambit of a criminal prosecution for such crimes; lastly, there has been the Cour de Cassation's decision to give a broad 'interpretation' to the concept of crimes against humanity. In one way or another, especially while the socialists were in government, the *premises were laid* for the calm re-examination of past guilt, as well as of future 'deviations'. Above all, in cases where *raisons d'Etat* can run counter to humanitarian values, the *principal role* has been passed on (as

is right) to private groups, private individuals and to the press
(as well as to all organizations that enjoy, under French law,
the right to 'spur' the state). In future, *they* will have to make
sure that the government and all its agencies respect the
supreme 'decalogue' of human rights. Proof of how effective is
the role of the private citizen emerged in 1965. That year US
intelligence decided to put Barbie back on their books. This
decision came to naught because an American lady wrote to
her senator, Jacob Javits, after watching a television pro-
gramme on the 'easy life' of numerous war criminals. She asked
him to inquire whether the US government still employed the
services of ex-Nazi criminals. Javits passed on her letter to the
State Department. This was enough to convince the CIA that
theirs was a risky operation, and that they should cancel it.

Fortunately, in France as in other democratic countries,
there is no lack of individuals and private organizations that
will not allow governments to go their solitary way, forgetting
that the 'human condition' requires respect for rights they
frequently choose to ignore.

8

Abraham and Antigone
Two conflicting imperatives

To the two German soldiers, shot because they refused to join in the massacre at Marzabotto.[1]

Abraham and Antigone: two archetypes

In the *Book of Genesis* we are told that God called Abraham and ordered him to take his son, Isaac, and go with him into the land of Moriah and offer him there as a burnt sacrifice. Abraham obeyed: he saddled his ass, called Isaac and two young servants, gathered wood for the sacrifice and went unto the place God had commanded him. When, after three days, they came to the mountain, he told the young men to wait, loaded Isaac with the wood, took torch and knife and together they walked up towards the appointed place. Isaac then asked where the sacrificial lamb was; Abraham answered that God would provide the lamb. When they came to the place, Abraham built an altar, laid the wood for the pyre, bound Isaac and set him on the altar and took the knife to slay him. Then, and only then, did the Angel of the Lord stay his hand ('Now I know that thou fearest God, seeing thou hast not withheld thy son, thine only son from me'). So runs the story in Genesis.[2]

Commentators dwell on how cruel a test God expects Abraham to pass to prove his faith. But there is something even more striking in this biblical tale. After receiving God's command, Abraham shows no hesitation in carrying it out: the most cruel command imaginable, one that contravenes all the laws of humanity and ethics: to kill his own son, his 'only' son. Yet Abraham never rebels, never wonders whether the command is just, never berates a God who has forced him to commit such a wicked act. Except that he lacks the courage to tell Isaac he is himself the sacrificial victim and answers his query with a linguistic wile, avoiding the question and concealing the truth. Indeed, Abraham is the archetype of the man who 'obeys authority blindly', as the saying goes, who never for a moment questions the order imparted; he is the archetypal yes-man.

At the opposite extreme is Antigone. Two of her brothers have killed one another; one, Polynices, had led the assault on Thebes; the other, Eteocles, had defended the city. Creon, king of Thebes, forbids the burial of the former because he had tried to 'burn and destroy his fatherland' and rebelled against the power that held sway in the city where he was born. Creon wishes to inflict a punishment such as will be remembered by all those who spread 'anarchy' and try to 'demolish the houses', because 'great honour is given to him who upholdeth his country's laws'. As the sister of the two dead men, Antigone decides to disobey Creon's command: her love for her brothers, as well as the 'unchangeable' and 'eternal' laws that require us to bury the dead, she feels, override the orders of the authorities. Creon then condemns her to life imprisonment and Antigone kills herself. This, in essence, is the heart of one of Sophocles' most beautiful tragedies, one in which Antigone stands for all those who break the laws of the establishment to obey more humane imperatives. Antigone is the archetype of those who, caught in the dichotomy between an order from the powers that be and respect for higher values, choose the latter, knowing full well that they will be made to pay for their choice. It is no accident that Antigone is a woman. At the beginning of the tragedy, her sister Ismene refuses to connive in breaking the 'laws of the sovereign' and reminds Antigone 'we are women; it is not for us to fight against men; our rulers are stronger than we, and we must obey in this, or in worse than this.' However, Antigone is firmly resolved to commit 'a holy crime'. Whosoever has to bear oppression day by day, but does so with moral strength and fighting spirit, is more easily led to revolt against a single injurious act, the last of a host of iniquities.

Abraham and Antigone are the mythic emblems of two possible 'answers' to 'superior orders'. Myth and poetry show, in sublimated and dramatic idiom, two kinds of reaction, both of them 'human', to the injunctions of rulers; they illustrate the alternatives 'invented' by mankind to solve a conflict that, in either case, must end in tragedy. But are these the only possible 'answers', or have people in their daily lives contrived other solutions? And has law perhaps proposed other ways to solve the terrible dilemma? We all know that during the last world war orders were given that were contrary to the most elementary respect for human dignity and that, later on, those who had carried them out, on being required to account for their actions before the tribunals (of their ex-enemies), excused their acts by claiming to have obeyed superior 'orders'. What did the tribunals ordain? Whom did they uphold, Abraham or Antigone? And how should we judge them today? Above all, how are we to behave if we receive an order (from a political ruler or a military superior) which we feel is contrary to moral tenets and to the highest legal imperatives?

Obedience in a democratic state: Milgram's experiments

Before taking a look at how 'law' responds to these questions, let us glance at how things work in effect, in our day-to-day lives. From this point of view, the experiments of an American psychologist Stanley Milgram, carried out between 1960 and 1963 on adults in the New Haven area of Connecticut,[3] are extremely helpful. Bearing in mind how during the Second World War numerous Nazis, on orders from their superiors, took part in wholesale persecution and slaughter, Milgram wanted to test, in rigorous experiment, the mechanism that induces individuals to inflict pain on others and discover to what extent we are conditioned by the 'commands' of our superiors. The technique he used in the experiments was quite simple: adults taken from different social classes and of differing cultural backgrounds were invited to the Yale laboratory to take part in a study on 'memory and learning'. The test, it was explained, was meant to ascertain the effects of punishment on learning. A 'learner' (an actor, though the person taking part in the experiment did not know this) was seated with his hands tied and electrodes attached to his wrists. His task was to memorize a list of verbal associations. The real subject of the experiment, the 'teacher', was taken into the room where the 'learner' was sitting and seated in front of an enormous generator with push buttons. His task was to make sure the 'learner' made the correct answers to his questions on verbal associations. For every wrong answer he had to administer an electric shock, starting with the lowest voltage and increasing steadily. The 'instructor' (one of the psychologists taking part in the experiment), dressed in a white coat, gave orders to the 'teacher' whenever the latter hesitated or refused to push the button to give the 'learner' a shock after a wrong answer. Naturally, the 'learner's' ability to memorize was a pretext; the real object of the test was to see to what extent the 'teacher' would inflict pain on the 'learner' obeying the 'instructor's' order.

Milgram's experiments proved beyond doubt that, despite the atrocious pain the 'learner' felt (or pretended to feel), in over half the cases the subject of the experiment continued to administer the shocks. As Milgram remarked:

> The results, as seen and felt in the laboratory, are . . . disturbing. They raise the possibility that human nature, or – more specifically – the kind of character produced in American democratic society, cannot be counted on to insulate its citizens from brutality and inhumane treatment at the direction of malevolent authority. A substantial proportion of people do what they are told to do, irrespective of the content of the act and without limitations of conscience, so long as they perceive that the command comes from a legitimate authority.[4]

How can these results be accounted for? Milgram and other psychologists have underscored the essentially authoritarian role of the family, the school, the Church and the place of work; all these 'communities' instil in the individual respect for authority, the duty to bow to 'superior' orders, relieving his conscience from any sense of responsibility (from the earliest age when a father tells his child not to beat up children of his own age, not only is he teaching him the duty to respect others, but transmitting another 'hidden' message: a father must be obeyed by his child; this message becomes even more imperious, though more contradictory, when the father beats his child because it has beaten up other children). The interiorization of the hierarchical structure of the social groups in which we live helps us to accept orders even in 'conflictual situations', such as when we discover that by carrying out an order we inflict pain on others.

This socio-psychological context, with its serious consequences for national communities that are otherwise democratic, is obviously exasperated in authoritarian structures, such as the *armed forces* and, on a larger scale, in autocratic states.

These rapid observations should be borne in mind now that I am about to examine the 'response' of law, to inquire how realistic it is and, therefore, to what extent it is capable of guiding human conduct *effectively*.

Military structures and the question of subordinates

In the international community the question of 'superior orders' has often been posed, but only or almost exclusively in relation to *military structures* and in case of *war*: when military commanders have told their subordinates to perform acts that were in fact criminal. What was the subordinate to do? He was faced with an awful dilemma: military discipline is based on obedience and on a scrupulous respect for orders from one's superiors; if a subordinate were to question and dispute an order, what would happen to discipline and relations between superiors and inferiors and to the military structure itself? On the other hand, may a soldier carry out an order passively, even though it obviously contradicts not only the most elementary moral tenets, but also the legal rules that regulate social relations? The subordinate is, therefore, trapped between dramatic alternatives – all the more serious because he is at war and, by carrying out an obviously criminal order, he may be punished by the enemy. In more general terms, the great English constitutionalist, A. V. Dicey,[5] observed that a soldier is obviously caught in a grievously conflictual situation:

> The position of a soldier is in theory and may be in practice a difficult one. He may, as it has been well said, be liable to be shot by a court-martial if he disobeys an order, and to be hanged by a judge and jury if he obeys it.

The problem becomes even more complex with the addition of other circumstances: for instance, what should be done if an officer tells a soldier to shoot some prisoners of war and, when his subordinate hesitates, draws a pistol and threatens to shoot him if he does not obey? To such instances of physical or 'moral' coercion one may add cases of 'ignorance of the facts' by an inferior. For example, an officer tells a soldier to shoot an enemy civilian and, when the latter wavers, explains that the civilian had illegally taken part in belligerent activities, thereby committing the war crimes for which he had been regularly tried; after the execution it is revealed that the officer had lied; in such circumstances can one hold that the soldier is also guilty?

These cases – none of them invented, because they all happened in fact – are further complicated by others. But it serves no purpose to add to the list. Let us now see how law 'responded'. Since it is formed by people under the impulse of both practical needs and the dictates of morality, let us see how law reacted to these two sources.

The 'old' law begins to crack

For centuries the principle of obedience to hierarchical superiors has held sway. Eichmann, speaking before the District Court of Jerusalem, called it 'the cadaver's obedience' (*Kadavergehorsam*), using an expression that echoed the well-known dictum of the Jesuits. The reason why obedience went unquestioned for so much of history was that people believed army discipline and passive obedience were intrinsic to military life. The corrosive acid of the doctrine of human rights had not yet eaten into these principles, suggesting the virtue of insubordination to orders that seem contrary to human dignity. For centuries, therefore, whenever responsibility for criminal acts had been detected and punished, this responsibility had belonged entirely to the *officers* who imparted the criminal order: the executors were protected by the maxim *respondeat superior*.

Leafing through legal decisions and the practice of states, the first example we find of a flaw in the principle of passive obedience comes from the United States. During the Civil War (1861–5), Captain Henry Wirz, a Swiss doctor who had emigrated to Louisiana and, 'carried away by the maelstrom of excitement' (as he was to write later), had joined the Confederate army of the Southern states, was given the command of a prison camp in Andersonville (Georgia). Here he contravened the current laws of war and maltreated the prisoners, keeping tens of thousands of Unionist soldiers in inhuman conditions; some of these were even tortured and killed (the statements of the 'survivors' and the eye-witness accounts given at Wirz's trial remind one of an *ante litteram* Rudolf Hoess – though, Hoess obviously had far more 'refined' means at his disposal in Auschwitz, as well as extremely efficient medical, bureaucratic and military assistance). In 1865, when the war was over, Wirz was tried by a military commission in Washington; he defended himself by saying he had acted on superior orders, because he had been merely 'a medium, or better, a tool in the hands of his superiors'. At this point the judge advocate objected that when an order is illegal, both the superior officer and his subordinate are guilty. His exact words were:

I know that it is urged [by the defense] that during all this time he was acting under General Winder's orders, and for the purpose of argument I will concede that he was so acting. A superior officer cannot order a subordinate to do an illegal act, and if a subordinate obey such an order and disastrous consequences result, both the superior and the subordinate must answer for it. General Winder could no more command the prisoner to violate the laws of war than could the prisoner do so without orders. The conclusion is plain, that where such orders exist both are guilty, and *a fortiori* where the prisoner at the bar acted upon his own motion he was guilty.

The commission accepted this argument and condemned Wirz to death by hanging. The execution, confirmed by President Johnson, took place on 11 November 1865.[6]

For a full understanding of the reasons behind this early breach in the solid edifice of military requirements one should remember that the trial was held by the victors against the vanquished, as well as the nature of the crimes attributed to Wirz. I feel it is apposite here to recall the distinction B. V. A. Röling, the great Dutch jurist, drew between two categories of war crimes. There is 'individual criminality', that is crimes committed by a single man (killing old people and children, rape, plunder, and so on); and 'system criminality', that is crimes of a collective nature: these are the unlawful acts of soldiers or officers, performed at the instigation or on the orders of the whole military structure and, if not of the political establishment itself, at least with the wholehearted approval of the state authorities; acts that include the use of forbidden weapons, the systematic bombing of a civilian population, large-scale maltreatment of prisoners, and so on. In the first case, the criminal act is the expression of the violent impulses of one man, seen by the army to which he belongs as a dishonourable act that discredits the whole armed forces; he is then punished without delay by the courts of his native country. On the other hand, 'system criminality', that is the actions of one man, dictated or approved by the whole collectivity, is punished – if ever – only by the *enemy* and only when the latter has *won* the war.[7]

Now, if we apply this essential distinction in the light of the historical facts at our disposal, it would appear that the case of Captain Wirz was one of 'system criminality'. The military commission in Washington only broke with the traditional principle *respondeat superior* because, as I have already noted, Wirz was a *former enemy*.

The next breach in the traditional respect for superior orders takes us right up to the First World War. In 1915 Fryatt, the British commander of the merchant vessel *Brussels*, flying the Union Jack, crossed the path of a German submarine, which ordered him to heave to and identify himself. Instead of obeying, Fryatt, on orders from the Admiralty to all merchant vessels in similar circumstances, bore down at full speed on the enemy submarine and tried to ram it. The submarine moved off to avoid collision and Fryatt got away. On another voyage, however, the *Brussels* was captured and Fryatt tried and condemned for war crimes (he was regarded as a *franc tireur*, that is an unlawful combatant) even though he had merely been carrying out superior orders.[8] The British commander's criminal action belonged to the category of 'system criminality'. His obvious violation of the laws of war (which only allowed members of the armed forces and a few other circumscribed categories of combatants to take part in the hostilities) and the fact that Fryatt was tried *by the enemy*, explains why the Germans ignored the circumstances that he had obeyed instructions from the British Admiralty.

However, after the war the Germans continued along the same lines, taking no notice of superior orders in a series of trials against German soldiers held before the Supreme Court in Leipzig (the Allies had wanted to try the Germans who had violated the laws of war, but for various political reasons the importance of these trials deflated and the job was handed over to a German tribunal, the Leipzig Court).

Of the Leipzig trials let me recall briefly those that are outstanding from our present point of view: the 'Dover Castle' and 'Llandovery Castle' cases.[9]

Underlying both cases was the Allied practice of using hospital ships for belligerent purposes (that is to transport munitions and troops), contrary to the laws of war. In 1917, to put an end to this practice, the German Admiralty had officially requested the Allied commanders of hospital ships to comply with the regulations, if they wished the Germans to respect their immunity. As it had not obeyed the German directives, the British hospital ship 'Dover Castle' was attacked and sunk by a German submarine whose commander, Karl Neumann, assured the Court in Leipzig that he had acted on orders from the German Admiralty. The Court decided – quite rightly – that Neumann had every right to believe those orders had been legitimate and that his actions were merely a reprisal against the British. Thus, Neumann could not be condemned, because article 47 of the German military penal code of 1872 only foresaw the punishment of a subordinate who carried out an order when that order was illegal, or when he overstepped the limits of that order. Although the Court did not declare the accused guilty, it did rule on the general principle that a subordinate is responsible for his acts if these are criminal, even when he is acting on the orders from his superiors.

In applying the same domestic law and the same general principle, the Court reached a different conclusion in the 'Llandovery Castle' case. This was also a British hospital ship, but it was illegally sunk because it was not in the area covered by the instructions of the German Admiralty. In this case Patzig, the commander of the German submarine, first sunk the ship and then ordered three of his officers to fire on the three lifeboats the English had launched, to remove all trace of the illegal sinking. Patzig disappeared after the war, but two of the three officers (Dithmar and Boldt) were arrested and tried. Naturally, they told the Leipzig court that they had merely carried out Patzig's orders. However, the Court turned down their plea and stated that the orders had clearly been unlawful because they contravened the laws of war. The Court stressed among other things, that so as not to have witnesses, Patzig had made his crew go below deck before he started to shoot the survivors; besides, the day after the sinking, he summoned his crew and asked them not to mention the shelling of the lifeboats, for which 'he, alone, would answer before God and his own conscience'; he did not enter the events in his log book; and, unluckily for him, the survivors on one of the lifeboats had been picked up and had denounced him.

The importance of this decision (for the first time a state court had condemned its *own nationals* for obeying an unjust order) is however reduced by three facts. First, the Leipzig trials were to a certain extent 'forced' on Germany by the victorious Allies. Second, Dithmar's and Boldt's offences were clear examples of 'individual criminality'. Third, the Leipzig trials were, in general, far from exemplary on the practical plane (the few offenders whose guilt was recognized were given ridiculously light sentences and almost all escaped from their respective prisons, apparently with the complicity, or at least under the blind eye of the German authorities). However, in our particular case the fact remains that the sentence rejected the principle *respondeat superior*. If we are to appreciate its importance, we must remember that in the past the prevailing rule had always been that of *passive obedience*: this decision, together with the others I have briefly summarized, are all happy exceptions, the first signs of a tendency that was just beginning to emerge. We must remember that the rules applying to the British and American armed forces at that time punished *only the superior officers* who had given the criminal orders; they completely exonerated their subordinates from any responsibility. Thus, two such civilized countries as Britain and the United States, together with the rest of the international community, still allowed the exigencies of military discipline to prevail.

Nuremberg: a turning point

Things changed drastically during the Second World War. The massacre of civilians and prisoners of war, the persecution of the Jews, the gypsies and political opponents, had become a large-scale phenomenon. Above all, this was a *'policy' pursued by the highest Nazi echelons* (and on a lesser scale by the Italian fascists and the Japanese) with predetermination and perseverance, and applied by the whole military and bureaucratic apparatus. (One of the most ruthless Nazi criminals, Hans Frank, responsible for persecutions and massacres in Poland, and subsequently justly condemned to death, declared, with a sudden flash of guilt to the Tribunal in Nuremberg: 'We have fought against Jewry; we have fought against it for years. And we have allowed ourselves to make utterances – and my own diary has become a witness against me in this connection – utterances which are terrible . . . A thousand years will pass and this guilt of Germany will not be erased'.)[10]

Collective criminality became possible because there existed an efficient bureaucratic structure, founded on a scrupulous respect for 'superior orders' and thus on order and discipline. It was the very existence of this modern administrative machinery that made the 'banality of evil' (H. Arendt)[11] possible, with the most inhuman directives being carried out promptly and efficiently. Thus we had the rapid, 'perfect' construction of concentration camps; the impeccable transport by rail of civilians and prisoners of war to forced labour camps; the meticulous bureaucratic slaughter of thousands and thousands of Jews. The whole military and bureaucratic apparatus, as well as the German population itself, obeyed and kept silent (fortunately there were exceptions: among these the bishop M. Niemöller and the 'White Rose' group). All the directives came from above and everyone obeyed them: it is the *Führerprinzip*, a monstrous hypertrophy of the maxim *respondeat superior*, which was made possible by the pyramidal structure of the totalitarian state and by the systematic elimination of any pocket of political and moral resistance. The crimes requested by the directives of the dictator and the Nazi leaders naturally belong to 'collective or system criminality': such was their nature that it would have been impossible to punish them by using the courts of the state to which the perpetrators belonged. Only an adversary could have made sure that justice was done, after first winning the war, that is.

Thus the Allies felt duty bound to find a new remedy. Since the criminal actions had spilled over from the traditional offences (war crimes) into an area that had previously been protected by the tenets of morality and respect for human dignity (or at least diplomatic prudence), there was now the unhappy need to 'invent' *new juridical categories*: those of 'crimes against humanity' (racial, religious or political persecution; the extermination or deportation of non-enemy populations, for example the populations of allies) and of 'crimes against peace' (wars of aggression; criminal plans to attack peace-abiding states).

But this was not enough. The *Führerprinzip* and the postulate that every order must be carried out without fail (*Befehl ist Befehl*, or an order is an order: what a sinister tautology!), can create an *unsurmountable barrier*, protecting the thousands of politicians, industrialists, bureaucrats and military men who at all levels applied to varying effect, but almost always with zeal, the Führer's inhuman directives. It was essential to shatter this barrier. The colossal scale at which *systematically criminal* political directives were *passively* carried out, *en masse*, required that the Allies adopt radical measures, tailored to the enormity of what had gone on. Great Britain, and then the United States, both modified their military regulations in 1944, substituting the rule *respondeat superior* with another: if an order is illegal, both the superior officer who gave it and its executor are responsible. However, the decisive step had to be taken at an international level. Thus, between 1943 and 1945, the United Nations War Crimes Commission, made up of seventeen Allied countries, laid down a specific norm (among other rules) based on the American and Soviet suggestions. Later, this rule became the famous article 8 of the Statute of the International Military Tribunal of Nuremberg (1945), which provides as follows: 'The fact that the defendant acted pursuant to order of his Government or of a superior shall not free him from responsibility, but may be considered in mitigation of punishment if the Tribunal determine that justice so requires'.

Not unexpectedly, during the trial before the International Tribunal in Nuremberg, the Nazi defence invoked the *Führerprinzip* and pleaded that the accused had always acted on orders from the supreme head of state. As Nelte, one of the counsels for the defence, stated, the accused had been 'merely mouthpieces or tools of an overwhelming will'.[12] But the Tribunal rejected these explanations. In referring to the *Führerprinzip*, it noted:

Hitler could not make aggressive war by himself. He had to have the co-operation of statesmen, military leaders, diplomats, and business-men. When they, with knowledge of his aims, gave him their co-operation, they made themselves parties to the plan he had initiated. They are not to be deemed innocent because Hitler made use of them, if they knew what they were doing. That they were assigned to their tasks by a dictator does not absolve them from responsibility for their acts. The relation of leader and follower does not preclude responsibility here any more than it does in the comparable tyranny of organized domestic crime.[13]

The Tribunal also dismissed another objection: that the defendants had acted on orders that conformed to the *laws* of the *whole* German military and bureaucratic structure – in other words, the *whole German legal system* required such conduct and they had felt duty bound to obey. On this point the Tribunal remarked that: 'the very essence of the Charter [of the Tribunal] is that individuals have international duties which transcend the national obligations of obedience imposed by the individual state'.[14]

To be more specific, the Tribunal applied the rigorous precepts contained in article 8 of its Statute, adding, however, one qualification that in which a subordinate did not have 'moral choice'.[15] According to the most plausible interpret-ation, the Tribunal intended this somewhat unclear concept to emphasize the fact that the judges must always bear in mind not only the superior orders, but other circumstances too; for example, duress (the commanding officer forces a subordinate to carry out an order at pistol point), or errors of fact (think of the case I mentioned earlier, where a civilian is shot by a soldier who had been told by his officer that the man had had a regular trial and had been sentenced).

However, the important point is that the International Tribunal – in general and also in the specific cases of Keitel and Jodl, when it ruled on the plea of superior orders – clearly rejected the exceptions advanced by the defence and declared it the duty of a subordinate to refuse to carry out a criminal order (except in the circumstances I have just mentioned).

The judgement of the Nuremberg Tribunal, later reiterated by the International Tribunal in Tokyo, is one of the highest points ever reached by the new juridical conscience. Until that moment, individuals had to obey the imperatives of their own national laws and, more specifically, they had to obey the orders of their superior officers, even when these were contrary to the most elementary moral tenets and to the humanitarian rules that had crystallized in international law. Up to that time the *exceptions* (already mentioned earlier) had been very few and far between. Not only did the Nuremberg Tribunal proclaim that a 'superior order' must be disregarded if it is contrary to national law, it also laid down that – for the first time in history – when the *international rules* that protect humanitarian values are in conflict with *state laws* that contravene those values, *every individual must transgress the state laws* (except where there is no room for 'moral choice'). This was a veritable revolution, both in the field of law and of ethics. But what was its effect thereafter? Was its impact limited by the fact that the verdict had been given by the victors against the vanquished? How many other states and peoples took up the torch, and how many remained anchored to old principles of state sovereignty?

Decisions of national courts

If we take a look at the post-war judgements of the American Tribunal in Nuremberg (not to be confused with the International Tribunal), which operated in the American military zone from 1946 to 1949, as well as the decisions of the victorious (or almost victorious) nations such as Britain, France, the Netherlands, Norway, Italy, not to mention the Eastern European countries (the USSR and Poland, for example), it becomes clear that the principles applied in Nuremberg by the International Tribunal were never questioned but reiterated, spelt out and broadened. In fact, the courts asserted unequivocally that a subordinate must refuse to carry out an illegal order, the only possible justification being that he was forced to do so (or was misinformed by errors of fact). In reasserting the principle of what the French call 'intelligent bayonets', the courts wavered, however, between two different interpretations. In some cases the 'objective' criterion of the *obviously criminal* nature of the superior order was applied; in other cases a more 'subjective' criterion was preferred: the subordinate was guilty if he *was* (*or should have been*) *aware* of the criminal nature of the order. But these variations were unessential and left the substance of the principle unchanged.

Out of a stack of cases I shall mention only a few, choosing those I feel are most significant.

One of the cases brought before the American Tribunal in Nuremberg was the *Einsatzgruppen* case.[16] These were 'action groups' created in 1941 by two sinister Nazi organizations, the Sicherheitsdienst (security services) and the Sicherheitspolizei (security police), to carry out a double job in territories occupied by the German army: police functions (especially in the anti-partisan war), and the 'liquidation' of Jews, gypsies and political opponents. Most of all the *Einsatzgruppen* distinguished themselves by their pitiless extermination of Jews. However, in the Nuremberg Court the accused, who were all members of these 'groups', were so brazen as to invoke 'superior orders'.

The Court remarked that admittedly, to be efficient, all military structures must insist on military discipline, which means that soldiers are duty-bound to obey. But this obedience must not be blind:

> It is a fallacy of widespread consumption that a soldier is required to do everything his superior officer orders him to do. A very simple illustration will show to what absurd extreme such a theory could be carried. If every military person were required, regardless of the nature of the command, to obey unconditionally, a sergeant could order the corporal to shoot the lieutenant, the lieutenant could order the sergeant to shoot the captain, the captain could order the lieutenant to shoot the colonel, and in each instance the executioner would be absolved of blame. The mere statement of such a proposition is its own commentary . . . The obedience of a soldier is not the obedience of an automaton. A soldier is a reasoning agent. He does not respond, and is not expected to respond, like a piece of machinery.

My other case concerns the *High Command*.[17] Among the defendants were high-ranking officers in the German army accused of having taken part in various ways in war crimes, crimes against humanity or against peace. They had either ordered criminal acts, or they had taken an active part in devising and planning these actions, or they had endorsed or even passively transmitted Hitler's orders and those of other top Nazi leaders. Among other pleas, the defendants pointed out that Hitler became the High Commander of the German armed forces in 1938 and, therefore, his orders had to be obeyed by his subordinates, especially by those of highest military rank such as the accused. Among the orders given by Hitler, or by his closest collaborators, they mentioned the 1941 directive on the execution without trial of Soviet political commissars; the infamous 'Barbarossa' order given by Keitel, also in 1941, on shooting without trial partisans and other enemy civilians fighting the invading German troops; also the subsequent 1941 decree, issued by Hitler with Keitel's signature, called 'Night and Fog' (*Nacht und Nebel*), on the summary execution of 'non-German civilians' who had committed offences against the German forces of occupation; Hitler's 1942 order for the summary execution of sabotage commandos, and so on.

The Court rejected the defence's pleas, though it did take note that some of the defendants (Wilhelm von Leeb among others) had somehow opposed Hitler's orders, or had put off or circumscribed their execution. However, the Court was very firm in applying the principle, adding new reasons to those adduced in previous cases. It stated it would have been absurd to declare Hitler alone to be guilty of all the misdeeds. It added that the directives and orders quoted by the defence were all contrary to international law (which, among other points, insists that there always be a trial against civilians or soldiers accused of crimes against the occupying forces). The Court went on as follows:

> The defendants in this case who received obviously criminal orders were placed in a difficult position, but servile compliance with orders clearly criminal for fear of some disadvantage or punishment not immediately threatened cannot be recognized as a defense. To establish the defense of coercion or necessity in the face of danger there must be a demonstration of circumstances such that a reasonable man would apprehend that he was in such imminent physical peril as to deprive him of freedom to choose the right and refrain from the wrong. No such situation has been shown in this case.

It further buttressed its view by remarking that not only did article 47 of the German military criminal code (which I have already had occasion to mention) punish those who carried out illegal orders, but in 1940 this rule had been modified such that the duty of a subordinate not to carry out a criminal order had been strengthened. Ironically, in 1944, Goebbels (then minister for propaganda) speaking of Allied pilots, had taken the opportunity to write the following on military duties: 'No law of war provides that a soldier will remain unpunished for a hateful crime by referring to the orders of his superiors, if their orders are in striking opposition to all human ethics, to all international customs in the conduct of war.'[18]

Another famous case is the *Peleus'*, adjudicated by a British military court in Hamburg (in the British military zone) in 1945.[19] The facts resembled those of the 'Llandovery Castle' case. The *'Peleus'*, a Greek merchant vessel serving the British, had been torpedoed by a German submarine under the command of Captain Eck. The ship did not sink at once and various members of the crew were able to cling to two rafts and to the shipwrecked vessel. The submarine surfaced and the commander and four officers shot at the shipwrecked sailors, killing many of them. At the trial, the counsel for the defence of the four officers said they were not responsible because they had been carrying out Eck's orders. Turning to the Court the judge advocate rebutted this plea as follows:

It is quite obvious that no sailor and no soldier can carry with him a library of International Law, or have immediate access to a professor in that subject who can tell him whether or not a particular command is a lawful one. If this were a case which involved the careful consideration of questions of International Law as to whether or not the command to fire at helpless survivors struggling in the water was unlawful, you might well think it would not be fair to hold any of the subordinate accused in this case responsible for what they are alleged to have done; but is it not fairly obvious to you that if in fact the carrying out of Eck's command involved the killing of these helpless survivors, it was not a lawful command, and it must have been obvious to the most rudimentary intelligence that it was not a lawful command, and that those who did that shooting are not to be excused for doing it upon the ground of superior orders?

The Court accepted his arguments and sentenced all five of the defendants.

Finally, let me deal with a more recent case: Eichmann, who was tried and sentenced (1961–2) by the District Court of Jerusalem and by the Supreme Court of Israel for having organized the 'final solution' for the Jews.[20] Eichmann claimed he was a 'mere cog' in the monstrous machinery of Nazism.

However, at a certain stage, in answer to a question put by the District Court he admitted to having known about the criminal nature of his actions:

> I already realized at the time that this solution [to the Jewish question] by the use of force was something unlawful, something terrible, but to my regret I was obliged to deal with it in matters of transportation, because of my oath of loyalty [to the Führer] from which I was not released.

Both courts rejected his plea. The Supreme Court argued that, in fact, Eichmann had acted with complete independence:

> In point of fact, the appellant did not receive orders 'from above' at all; he was the high and mighty one, the commander of all that pertained to Jewish affairs . . . He was possessed by the concept of the 'final solution' and . . . did far more than was demanded or expected of him by his superiors in the chain of command.

The Court added that, even if it were agreed that Eichmann was 'carrying out orders', he could not hide behind the principle *respondeat superior*. Indeed, he was well aware, and it could not have been otherwise, of the highly criminal nature of his actions. Besides, there was no question of threats to his life had he not carried out the directives. It was quite untenable to say that he had acted out of necessity, or had been subjected to coercion. As we know, Eichmann was hanged.

This brief survey of post-war rulings shows that, in all the countries which held trials of Nazi war criminals, the courts upheld the principle of the *responsibility of subordinates*. I should add that after the war various states, which either drew up or rewrote their military manuals, all made explicit reference to superior orders and followed the new approach. I have already mentioned the American and British military manuals. These were both redrafted: the former in 1956 and the latter in 1958. Other nations to follow suit were the Federal Republic of Germany (1961), Israel and Switzerland (1963), Austria (1965) and the Netherlands (1974). As for other states, I can say nothing (except that the German Democratic Republic drafted its military manual in 1968, with an explicit rule on this subject)[21] because they either have no laws or manuals covering war, or because they are not accessible.

A more recent case: Lieutenant Calley

Thus, after the 1950s, the courts, the laws and military manuals unanimously (or almost unanimously) rejected the Nazi theory of passive obedience. However, it might be objected that these courts (and legislators) all belonged to the victorious powers and were judging soldiers and high-powered civil servants of defeated states. To what extent, one might ask, were the principles of a 'new international law', formulated between 1945 and 1950, considered binding by those same victorious powers? The question is a fair one because, as we all know, none of the courts I have referred to tried any of the very serious crimes committed by the Allies themselves (the indiscriminate bombing of many German and Japanese towns and the use of the atomic bomb).

In part I have already answered this query by quoting the numerous military manuals newly drafted, or updated, by many Western states (and the German Democratic Republic) from the 1950s onwards. But one case – particularly important because it concerns one of the two superpowers – proves that, as far as public opinion and certain sectors of the American Administration are concerned, the principles of Nuremberg are not dead and buried. This was the Calley case.[22] The facts are well known: on 16 May 1968 Lieutenant William L. Calley led a unit in an assault on My Lai, a village in South Vietnam, and killed about one hundred civilians. The massacre was kept secret. But, later, a courageous American soldier, Ronald Ridenhour, on learning by chance what had happened from some members of the 'expedition', felt duty bound to inform the Department of Defense so that an inquiry could be held. A short while later, Seymour M. Hersh, an American journalist who had heard rumours of the massacre, ferreted out the truth and soon My Lai was spread across the pages of the newspapers. The US Army decided to court-martial both Calley and some of his subordinate officers (who were immediately acquitted for reasons that are not at all clear) and Calley's commanding officer, Captain Medina. At the trial, among other things, Calley said that he had merely carried out Medina's orders: the latter had told him to consider all those he found in the village enemies and, therefore, to 'waste the people'. Medina denied having given these orders; when asked whether women and children were also to be killed, he apparently said common sense should be used, adding that it was admissible to shoot women and children if they had taken part in the hostilities or had tried to attack the American troops. Whatever the truth of the facts, the military judge whose 'job' it was to tell the members of the court martial what laws they were to apply, rejected the plea of superior orders, reiterating the main ideas that inspired the Nuremberg trials.

These concepts underlay the court martial's decision to consider Calley guilty: he was sentenced to life imprisonment. Naturally, he appealed. But the sentence was confirmed both by the Army Court of Military Review and by the Court of Military Appeals, although it was reduced to twenty years at the first appeal. The judgement of the second court of appeal was particularly interesting. Calley's defence had objected that, in weighing the responsibility of a soldier who had carried out an order, one should not adopt the criterion (followed by the court martial) that one must ascertain whether 'a man of ordinary sense and understanding' would have realized that the order was unlawful. Calley's counsel felt this criterion penalized the less intelligent soldiers, as well as those who were uninformed or inexperienced. They therefore suggested another criterion: that an order is unlawful when it is seen as such by 'a person of the commonest understanding'. They added that, since Calley was not particularly intelligent, he had not realized that the order to kill Vietnamese civilians was against the current laws. The majority of the Court rejected the plea. The judge who read out the majority opinion (R. E. Quinn) remarked that, even if it were possible to accept the plea, the final decision would remain unaffected: even a soldier of the lowest intellect, totally uninformed on points of military law, could not ignore the fact that to kill children and defenceless civilians was contrary to the most elementary principles of the laws of war.

Thus, the American judges applied the main ideas introduced in Nuremberg. The fact that, before the first appeal, President Nixon immediately ordered that Calley should be put on house arrest and not imprisoned, and that later, after the appeals and the reduction of his sentence, the President pardoned the lieutenant, casts an unfavourable light on the US Administration at that time. However, it does not detract from the importance of the judges' decisions. The judgement of the Calley case was all the more important since the My Lai massacre was one instance of the 'collective or system criminality' I mentioned earlier. This is proved among other things by the fact that the US Army tried to smother the 'episode'. It is important to remember (as the American general, Telford Taylor, himself asserted) that at the time the United States was pursuing a 'repressive' policy, leading to acts such as that for which Calley was justly condemned. (Indirect proof of this, among other points, was that in 1972, when the New York Bar requested Nixon to set up a 'national commission' to guard against the recurrence of another My Lai, the request was turned down in the President's name by one of his advisers. He explained that to accept the request would only have divided American public opinion further and, besides, an inquiry would have made public the 'rules governing the conduct of hostilities' for the American operations in Indo-China, which were and should remain a military secret. Telford Taylor's comment on this last justification was that orders and directives given to ensure a proper respect for the rules of war are effective only if the troops know and understand them; this was quite incompatible with military secrecy which, according to the President, should cover these orders and directives.)[23]

That the My Lai slaughter was a case of 'system criminality' makes the trial and sentence of an American officer by American military courts all the more significant. Furthermore, it is worth remembering here that quite a few American soldiers refused to take part in certain military operations to avoid becoming involved in criminal acts. A case in point was that of Captain Donald Dawson of the US Air Force. He was arrested for having refused to obey an order to undertake a mission with a B–52 bomber in Cambodia on 5 June 1973 (he said he was morally opposed to bombing Cambodia after the Paris agreements on Vietnam had been signed).[24] It is worth noting that in 1974 Dawson was released, after his right to be a conscientious objector had been recognized.

The upshot of all post-war case law

What can be deduced from my brief survey? The easiest conclusion, and one which many have already drawn, is that after the Second World War the profound indignation felt by the victorious nations at the *enormity* of what had been perpetrated, as well as the trials these countries did well to hold, led to a definite result on a legal plane: a general rule of international law emerged that was binding on all states. This was that subordinates are now held to be as responsible as their superiors when they carry out an obviously criminal act, that is one that is contrary to the essential rules of international law.

Let us pause a moment to examine this rule and ask ourselves if it is not too 'exacting' and therefore unrealistic. To demand that an inferior rebel against an illegal order – that is to demand that he not only is able to express his opinion on that order, but that he disobey, thereby taking a step that might cost him dear – may seem too much to ask, given the nature of military structures. Take, for example, Dicey's human dilemma, mentioned earlier. Can a subordinate be expected to sacrifice his career, his interests, perhaps his life as well, rather than obey an unlawful order? By so providing does the law demand that soldiers behave as heroes? I feel the 'answer' law gives to this question is less far-fetched and unrealistic than would seem at first glance. The rule on superior orders should be taken together with that on physical or 'moral' coercion, and that on errors of fact, mentioned earlier. If an officer obliges me, at gunpoint, to shoot a prisoner of war, I am not answerable for my act precisely because, in this case, the unlawful order was carried out under duress. I no longer have that 'moral choice' of which the International Tribunal of Nuremberg spoke; nor can I be expected to sacrifice my life rather than carry out an unjust order. As you see, law does remember that men are what they are and does not punish anyone who, forced to choose between his own life and that of another, prefers to save his own skin. Law does not expect us to behave as saints, martyrs or heroes, but it can demand that we risk a court martial, imprisonment and the sacrifice of a career, rather than carry out an obviously unlawful order.

These rules have marked an *extremely significant change of direction* in the international community. To a certain extent they have subverted military discipline. The imperatives of international law have seeped into the military structures of states, forcing soldiers to *disobey* their orders if they are contrary to international law and to the rulings that have been 'incorporated' into domestic law. Thus, the armour plating of state sovereignty has been torn at one of its most sensitive points: the hierarchical relations within a military structure. A man who carries out an obviously criminal order knows that he can be tried, sentenced and even put to death, either by court martial in his own country, or by a foreign court. At least in this area – but it is at the very 'heart' of the state – the humanitarian and progressive values contained in so many international rules have prevailed over the traditional 'impermeability' of military structures to the claims of the outside world. And that is a great step forward.

Yet, something is not quite right. This is not so much the gap, or even the strident difference, between this great advance along the road to civilization and the traditional closed structure of many states. Quite a different factor leaves us perplexed. If we take another look at the decisions and rules of the military manuals I mentioned, one fact stands out. They all belong to Western states, or to Eastern European states (as well as Yugoslavia). The Third World is absent, for obvious reasons. The majority of African and Asian states that now make up – at least from a numerical point of view – the backbone of the international community, were not yet independent immediately after the Second World War. Therefore, they could not express their views. For various historical reasons, the Latin American countries either did not have occasion, or did not wish, to hold trials against war criminals. After perusing the collections of decisions and the various military manuals, we have no idea of what their attitude is. In the absence of official statements from the Third World, can we say it considers itself bound by the general international rule on superior orders? We know well that the trauma of the crimes committed during the Second World War affected the consciences of all Western and socialist countries and led to their solemn pledge never to commit such horrors again and to the removal of that convenient loophole of 'superior orders'. Did it also affect Third World leaders?

This is not a strictly legal problem, but one of substance. Let me rephrase the question in other terms: can it be said that the Third World has also freed itself from an obsession with the *absolute principle* of *military discipline*? In the dichotomy between state sovereignty and international and humanitarian values, has it opted for the latter?

Alas, there is a whole pile of evidence that it hasn't, culled from debates in international organizations or at diplomatic conferences: in New York in 1948, and in Geneva in 1949 and then again in 1974–7.

The Third World challenges the right to disobey criminal orders

Negotiations for the Convention on Genocide

The first opportunity states had to express their opinion on the new rule was the preparatory work on the Convention on Genocide, which began in 1947 at the instigation of the United Nations.[25] In an *ad hoc* committee set up by the United Nations Economic and Social Council to make a draft of the Convention, the Soviet delegate suggested the introduction of a rule that reiterated the text proposed by the UN secretariat ('Command of the law or superior orders shall be no defence for crimes set out in this Convention, but may be considered in mitigation of punishment'). Of the other six members of the committee only the Pole gave his unconditional support to the Soviet proposal. The delegates from (Nationalist) China and Venezuela vigorously opposed it; their main reason for doing so was given by the Venezuelan as follows:

> that principle is a danger to the stability of the institutions of the state. The Charter of the Military Tribunal of Nuremberg admitted that principle having in mind the crimes of war; but to accept it in time of peace is to invite the armed forces to disobedience, when they are in themselves a non-political body, bound to obedience, and non-deliberative.[26]

There is no point in insisting here – as an Israeli scholar, Yoram Dinstein, did quite rightly a few years ago – that, in drawing a distinction between times of war and times of peace, the reasoning is fallacious (if there is a period of tension in which the exceptional nature of the moment could, to some extent, justify the requirements of military discipline, that is war; in times of peace 'there is no justification for sacrificing the supremacy of the law on the altar of military discipline').[27] Apart from these considerations, the significant point to be drawn from the Venezuelan argument is that a Third World country should have, for the first time, expressed its per-plexities and reservations on how the principle would affect the stability of state institutions. As we shall see, these are motives that later induced most developing countries to oppose the idea that a subordinate can legitimately disobey criminal orders.

However, the Soviet proposal was rejected, both at the committee level and, later, by the General Assembly of the United Nations, one of the reasons being that several Western countries (with the US to the forefront) added to the Latin American reservations (which dealt with general points and matters of principle) a whole set of marginal objections (for example, that the proposed rule was too 'rigid'; that the times were not ripe for a debate on superior orders; that the inclusion of the rule might impede the ratification of the Convention by some states, and so on). In any case, it was clear that the majority of states, especially Latin American and some Western countries, lacked the political will to accept a principle proposed and upheld by the same Western countries (and the Soviet Union) a few years earlier. The new Convention on Genocide, so important in some aspects and so weak and ambiguous in others, was born without one of its essential limbs: since acts of genocide are usually perpetrated by govern-ment authorities, or with their tacit support or connivance, genocide is a particularly fertile terrain for the principle *respondeat superior*.

Lawyers and diplomats who interpret the Convention are faced with a serious dilemma: in the absence of a specific rule on superior orders, is it possible, in suitable circumstances, to apply the general principle which several jurists felt had crystallized immediately after the Second World War? Or, does the rejection of the Soviet proposal mean that most of the states present in New York wished to rule out the responsibility of the subordinate in cases of genocide? This is still an open question.

Negotiations for updating the laws of war

What took place in New York in 1948 was repeated in Geneva in 1949 when the four famous Conventions on War Victims were discussed and approved; then again in 1974–7, when the two additional Protocols to these Conventions were drafted. Of these two occasions I feel the most significant was the second: it is closer to us in time and, above all, many more countries, especially non-Western ones, took part in the second lap of Geneva debates.[28] These debates give us a particularly revealing cross-section of the attitudes of various states, or groups of states, as well as their political and diplomatic motivations. Let us therefore take a look at the 1974–7 conference.

Once again a proposal had been made at the conference to insert a rule on superior orders into the First Additional Protocol (the one on international armed conflict, either between states or between states and national liberation movements). This time the proposal had been made not by a state, but by the International Committee of the Red Cross, which had drafted the basic texts on which the nations were to express their views. The rule (article 77) was wisely worded and introduced the question of superior orders into the wider context of a soldier's obedience to the hierarchy. It went as follows:

1 No person shall be punished for refusing to obey an order of his government or of a superior which, if carried out, would constitute a grave breach of the provisions of the Conventions or of the present Protocol.
2 The fact of having acted pursuant to an order of his government or of a superior does not absolve an accused person from penal responsibility if it be established that, in the circumstances at the time, he should have reasonably known that he was committing a grave breach of the Convention or of the present Protocol and that he had the possibility of refusing to obey the order.

Clearly, the rule sanctioned the *idea of superior orders* only for 'grave breaches' and did not extend it to 'ordinary' ones. Although this limitation was open to criticism, it was motivated by the fear that, otherwise, article 77 would not have been accepted by many countries. Despite the intentional lacuna, the rule was well drafted because it stated in clear terms the *logical premise* to the 'theory of superior orders', that is the *duty and right of the subordinate to refuse to obey*. What had always been *implicit* was now spelt out. But, precisely because the unsuppressible premise to the 'doctrine' was made patent, numerous governments rejected it firmly, in the belief that military discipline is one of the mainstays of the state and, consequently, it is one of the duties of a soldier to obey his orders without questioning them.

The proposal was the subject of lengthy and even bitter debate and, in the end, it foundered. But it is worth casting a rapid glance at the positions of states. For the sake of brevity, I shall ignore those that seem the least significant (either because they were isolated, or because they were based on ideas that were not shared by other delegations), as well as intermediate positions. In a nutshell, two main attitudes emerged: the one favourable to and the other against the rule.

The group of states that supported the rule, and in several cases suggested improvements to broaden its scope, included Western nations (Australia, Finland, the United States, Belgium, Norway, Canada, the Netherlands, Israel, Sweden, France, Japan, Ireland) and the Holy See, together with various socialist states (Poland, Ukraine, Yugoslavia, Cuba, the Socialist Republic of Vietnam) and a small group of Third World countries (Tunisia, the Philippines, Mexico).

Within this group, wholehearted support for article 77 came from the United States which, in 1976, suggested ammendments to improve the rule. In particular, the rule should be applicable to 'ordinary crimes' as well as 'grave breaches' – an extremely important suggestion, which eliminated one possible loophole and made article 77 even more consistent. Obviously, by 1976, the United States had changed its attitude and become one of the most ardent supporters of 'intelligent bayonets'.

The group of states that were substantially opposed to the principle of superior orders included various Arab states (Syria, Libya, Oman, United Arab Emirates, Kuwait, Yemen), as well as other developing nations (India, Ghana, the Republic of Korea). Briefly, to various extent and with varying attitudes, these countries felt extremely dubious, above all because they feared the rule would *lend legitimacy to insubordination*. This fear was expressed very adroitly by the Syrian and Indian delegates. In particular, the latter declared,

Article 77 . . . amounted to encouraging subordinates to disobey orders which they deemed contrary to the provisions of the Geneva Convention and Protocol I. The assumption was that Governments or superior officers would in some cases commit deliberate breaches of Protocol I. In such cases, whatever provisions might be inserted would remain inoperative.[29]

The war of words between the two groups ended in victory for the group that was opposed. Among other reasons, this was because some governments in the first group (such as the United States), preferred to vote against it after witnessing repeated attempts to water down article 77 and deprive it of its strength, believing that it was better to go home empty-handed than with an ill-conceived rule. Besides, they believed the Protocol would in no way impinge upon the general principle on superior orders, which they felt had crystallized after the Second World War.

What can be said of this final result? Certainly, the victors were state sovereignty and one of its mainstays, military discipline.

The countries to emerge victorious were those that feared that the 'free will' of subordinates was a powerful acid that would erode the efficiency of their military machines.

'In times no less than in regions there are wastes and deserts', as Bacon wrote in 1621.[30] From the beginning of the cold war to the present day, the supreme principles developed between 1945 and 1947 are desert bound. This has come about in spite of the birth of a new doctrine, foreshadowed by 'Nuremberg law': the 'doctrine of human rights', which has translated the natural law concept of 'human dignity' into positive legal rules and also underlies the concept of making subordinates 'responsible' for their actions. But, on closer inspection, even the acceptance of human rights by the Third World has been slow, it has come up against reticence, reservations and opposition and has often been accepted only begrudgingly. Military and political necessity in these countries, their need for strong, centralized administrations – a need that derives, in part, from their recent history – their respect for authoritarian ideologies and an excessive impermeability to values that, in the long run, would benefit the more backward societies, are all factors that help to explain the hostility of developing countries to any disruption of military discipline.

The deep rift in this area, as in others, would encourage a pessimist to think that we are witnessing the development of a 'two speed' law.

Conclusion

It is now time to haul our nets back into the boat and see how international law, that is states and their courts of law, has solved – if at all – the dilemma that first upset Abraham and Antigone, as well as thousands of men before, during and after the Second World War.

In these pages I have tried to show how, after that great conflagration, a conviction slowly crystallized in the international community that the duty to obey cannot cover the guilt of a soldier when essential values, such as respect for the life and dignity of a human being, are at stake. However, on closer examination, we discovered that an important sector of the international community had not contributed to that process of crystallization. Later, the Third World countries were able to express their opinion – true, not on the rule (or putative rule) directly, but on whether or not to draft provisions on limited issues that would reflect that rule.

It is for jurists *emunctae naris* – for exegetes and commentators – to discuss whether the attitude of developing countries proves that the rule never crystallized in fact; or that it did do so but, later, the hostility of a vast number of states splintered and weakened it; or, again, that the rule itself is hale and hearty, but some states are dubious about its applicability to certain areas. I, for one, feel it is important to highlight the *actual* behaviour of 'traditional' and emerging states on various occasions. Despite 'resistances' that, as Milgram's experiments showed, exist even in democratic states, where obedience to authority is no less radicated than in authoritarian states, immediately after the Second World War the victorious nations managed to introduce the principle that a soldier must not obey orders like a robot. Furthermore, they also proclaimed a 'concept' that I should like to emphasize once again: a soldier must disobey not only an order that transgresses the legislative dictates of his mother country, but – when the *whole texture of state laws has been infected* – he must even disregard orders that conflict with *extra-state commands*, that is the humanitarian values embodied in international law. Thus, *international law* has made a gigantic stride forwards compared to the psycho-social life of states, including democratic states. In spite of momentary hesitations, almost all Western and socialist states have stood firmly by those principles. Conversely, the majority of newly independent states have turned in the opposite direction; obsessed as they are with military necessity and security, they reject the idea that a soldier can challenge the orders of his superiors. In the end, these countries sacrifice to the requirements of authority the individual's independent judgement and his sense of personal responsibility. As far as they are concerned, there must be no Antigone.

The concepts that emerged from Nuremberg – one of the high points in our march towards legal civilization and an awareness of human dignity – are in danger of being silted up. What can be done? Should we wait until the authoritarian structure of many Latin American and Afro-Asian countries, based as they are on the force of arms and on the loyalty of troops, slowly open their portals to the canons of democracy? This process is likely to take years. Rather, public opinion should apply pressure, as from now, on the more enlightened sectors of the Third World to encourage these countries to realize that, in the long run, authoritarianism and oppression are always on the losing side. Indeed, however strong his imagery, Jean-Jacques Rousseau was wrong when he wrote in his *Discours sur l'origine et les fondements de l'inégalité parmi les hommes* that 'it is with liberty as it is with those solid and succulent foods, or with those generous wines, which are well adapted to nourish and fortify robust constitutions that are used to them, but ruin and intoxicate weak and delicate constitutions to which they are not suited.'[31] Perhaps jurists, as well as diplomats, could be of use by inventing in the various international forums better formulas that will lessen the diffidence of developing nations without diluting the essence of the principles that Antigone was the first to embody, paying for having transgressed Creon's orders with her life.

9

Front-line National Judges and International Law

The traditional safeguards of state sovereignty

When *foreign* states commit grave breaches of the law, the inertia of the government or its game of political compromise often induce national judges to take the law into their own hands. In such cases, these judges usually act at the behest of private individuals, whose possessions or interests have fallen victim to a foreign government. Domestic courts 'intervene' principally to protect private interests when it is feared the government will be too slow in acting or so conditioned by *raisons d'état* that it would tend to set aside the rights of individuals. Obviously, judges can act with greater freedom and effect than the administration, at least in those countries where there is a separation of powers, because they are not hobbled by reasons of political opportunity and the need to reconcile disparate interests such as shape the diplomacy of chancelleries. It is equally obvious that the latter see the action of domestic courts as undue interference in the conduct of foreign policy, which they regard as their exclusive preserve. This leads to friction and even to head-on collision, usually to the detriment of the individual.

Since governments dislike their domestic courts to interfere, they have tried to prevent such intrusions. Ever since the very beginnings of the international community, two rules have been created, designed to protect a government's independence and prevent domestic courts from emitting decisions on the behaviour of foreign states. Thus, the decision and possible 'conviction' are the special preserve of the respective chancelleries.

The first rule concerns a foreign state's exemption from jurisdiction: no state can be sued in the courts of another state for acts performed in its sovereign capacity, that is when it has acted as a governmental agency.

The second rule regards the 'immunity of state agencies': should an individual break the law of another state while acting as an agent for his country of origin and be brought before the state's courts, he is not held 'guilty' because he did not act as a private individual but as the representative of the state for which he acted. Like a minor, he is not liable. Only the state for which he acted can be 'called to account'. Once again the case is removed from the courts and submitted to the prudent and circumspect judgement of foreign ministries. One has only to quote some well-known 'cases' to give an idea of how these rules apply.

To illustrate immunity from jurisdiction let me mention only two cases, one heard in the House of Lords in 1938, the other examined by various Italian courts during the 1960s. The former, the *Cristina* case,[1] concerns a Spanish merchant vessel registered in Bilbao which sailed to Cardiff and was requisitioned at the behest of the Spanish consul (the Republican government in Madrid had issued a decree commandeering all private vessels for reasons of war, especially for the transport of goods, equipment and other merchandise needed in its war against the Franco forces). The ship's owners requested the British courts to state that they were the only legitimate proprietors. The Spanish government objected that it enjoyed immunity from jurisdiction and, therefore, the British courts had no say in the matter. The court of first instance, the Court of Appeal and the House of Lords all rejected the owners' plea. One of the judges, Lord Wright, analysed the reasoning behind the rule on immunity from jurisdiction and observed that it

> involves a subtraction from the sovereignty of the state, which renounces *pro tanto* the competence of its courts to exercise their jurisdiction even over matters occurring within its territorial limits, though to do so is *prima facie* an integral part of sovereignty. The rule may be said to be based on the principle *par in parem non habet imperium*, no state can claim jurisdiction over another sovereign state. Or it may be based on the circumstance that in general the judgement of a municipal court could not be enforced against a foreign state; or that the attempt to enforce might be regarded as an unfriendly act. Or it may

be taken to flow from reciprocity, each sovereign state within the community of nations accepting some subtraction from its full sovereingty in return for some similar concessions on the side of the others.

The other is the *Federici* case,[2] examined by various Italian courts from 1960 to 1968, ending up before the *Corte di Cassazione*. Giacomo Federici had numerous possessions in China; in September 1943 the Japanese troops that were occupying Shanghai requisitioned his moneys and goods to the value of $638,000. In 1947 the Japanese Liaison Office with the Commission for the Settlement of Allied Claims gave Federici a written statement recognizing his right to claim $638,000 from the Japanese state. Years passed while Federici wrestled with the bureaucratic procrastination of the Japanese administration, but not a dollar was forthcoming. Therefore, in 1959 he appealed to the Rome Tribunal, requesting it to force Japan to pay the compensation. Since the Japanese state did not put in an appearance, it was judged by default. On 8 July 1963 the Tribunal condemned Japan to pay the sum requested by Federici, observing that since in 1947 it had admitted his right to compensation, by a written statement recognizing the debt 'a typical private act' – it had acted like a private individual; this precluded Japan's immunity from jurisdiction. When the decision became final, Federici initiated various executive measures requesting the distraint by third parties of goods belonging to the Japanese state in Italy. At this stage the Administration intervened. The Prefect of Milan requested the *Corte di Cassazione* to declare that Italian courts could give no ruling on the matter because Japan, as a sovereign state, enjoyed complete immunity. At the same time, the Ministry of Foreign Affairs brought third party opposition against the Tribunal's decision: it claimed that Italian courts could not try a foreign state and only the government had the 'autonomous and exclusive right' to ensure that the issue were solved at an international level, via the usual diplomatic channels. Though rather late in the day, the reaction of the Administration was effective. Both the *Cassazione* and the Rome Tribunal decided that Italian courts could not condemn Japan. When the Japanese state had requisitioned Federici's possessions, it had acted as a sovereign state. The Tribunal added that relationships arising from acts of sovereignty performed by states (especially those relating to the activities of troops during military operations) can exist only and directly between states, as subjects of international law, even when these relationships concern damages caused to *individuals* and not to the state.

Consequently, in the opinion of the Tribunal, if the individual in question requests the municipal courts to decide on the matter, he not only impinges upon the sphere of action of the Ministry of Foreign Affairs, because he is trying to act in lieu of the state, but also damages other Italian citizens with similar claims, because his acts could jeopardize the diplomatic *démarches* of the Italian government on behalf of these claimants. In the end, Federici lost all along the line (although, as a result of an agreement between Italy and Japan in 1972, he finally obtained from the Italian Foreign Ministry what the Rome Tribunal had granted him in 1963).

As for the 'immunity of state agencies', the most celebrated example was the *McLeod* case of over one hundred years ago.[3] When Canada was still a British colony a rebellion broke out against the English. The rebels were assisted by American friends who used a ship, the *Caroline*, to transport arms, munitions and 'volunteers' across the Niagara, the river that forms the frontier between Canada and the United States. The British authorities were irritated and, in 1837, they sent Captain McLeod with an armed band to destroy the *Caroline* in the American port of Fort Schlusser, where it lay at anchor. The British expedition was successful, the ship was fired and set adrift in the direction of the famous falls. However, during the assault several American citizens were killed. Three years later McLeod went to New York where he was promptly arrested and accused of killing, together with others, several American citizens. McLeod told the Court in New York that he had acted on orders from the British government; the latter sent the Secretary of State, Webster, a note of protest, asserting that McLeod could not be tried because he had acted in an official capacity when he had attacked the *Caroline*. McLeod was let off, among other things for reasons of procedure similar to those according to which the New Zealand government hoped to end the imprisonment of two French secret service agents, who in July 1985 took part in an official mission to sink the

Rainbow Warrior in the port of Auckland during which a Dutchman lost his life. (In this case, however, the two were tried and convicted because the French government did not dare declare before the New Zealand court that the men had been acting on instructions from Paris.)[4] In the *McLeod* case the principle of the 'immunity of state agencies' was advanced and no one has questioned its applicability since. (Fortunately, there is one exception: international crimes, that is war crimes and crimes against peace and against humanity, for which responsibility falls not only to the state that ordered them, but also to the person who actually committed the crime).

This then is the 'legal framework' that stands in the way of a judge who would impinge upon the 'domestic affairs' of a foreign state with a ruling on actions which have offended the law of his own land. Clearly, both rules are based on one of the most effective principles in international law: reciprocity. It is the fear of 'retaliations' that makes municipal courts – or Foreign Ministries, as in the *Federici* case – stop any case that might prejudice the sovereign immunity of a foreign state.

Although the legal imperatives of international law have forced this straight-jacket on municipal courts, a few judges have, with some success, managed to *safeguard other legal and moral values worthy of greater respect than the 'dogma' of sovereignty*. In this essay I would like to draw your attention to the praiseworthy efforts of certain magistrates who have left the beaten path, showing courage and considerable imagination, to uphold other rights than those of the 'princes'.

The atomic bombing of Hiroshima and Nagasaki: the Shimoda case

In my view, one of the first outstanding decisions was that of the District Court of Tokyo in 1963.[5] Five survivors from Hiroshima and Nagasaki (the first of these was called Shimoda) initiated civil proceedings before the Tokyo Court to claim compensation for the damages they had suffered personally and for the deaths of their relations, killed during the bombing of the two cities. Naturally, they knew that if they wanted to obtain compensation for the international delict (the dropping of atomic bombs on Hiroshima and Nagasaki) they ought to have taken their case to an American court; they would have had to ask that court to rule that President Truman had violated international law and had thereby caused the five plaintiffs and the other Japanese victims incalculable damage. They also knew that American courts apply the so-called 'doctrine of the Executive's immunity': no US court can pronounce upon supreme acts of government, such as the decision to launch an atomic bomb. Consequently, Shimoda and his fellow plaintiffs brought their case against the Japanese state, not because it had caused the damage for which they claimed compensation, but because Japan had waived all claims on the United States both for itself and for its citizens in its 1951 Peace Treaty with the United States. According to Shimoda and his companions, by its renunciation Japan had violated the Japanese constitution, which confirms the citizens' right to have their property protected and, therefore, prohibits any waiving of compensation for an unlawful act. Thus, the Tokyo Court had to decide on an extremely complex tangle of domestic and international legal issues.

The compensation claimed by the plaintiffs was comparatively low: what they really wanted to achieve was not so much the payment of a sum of money as a *decision on the unlawful nature* of the atomic bombing of the two cities. In other words, they were aiming at a psychological and political victory. What they pursued was the legal, hence moral, condemnation of the bombing by a Japanese judge, at a time when the government had changed its attitude and now accepted the American point of view, declaring that in 1945 the United States had not violated the rules of international law.

As was to be expected, the Japanese government's line of defence was diametrically opposed to that of the plaintiffs. Thus, the Tokyo Court was called upon to decide both on the international law question and on various aspects of Japanese law. The 'preliminary' issue was obviously that of international law, because it was sufficient to solve the controversy: had the Court decided that the United States had not violated international law on 6 and 9 August 1945, the whole case would have collapsed. On the other hand, if the Court decided that the United States had disregarded one of the rules of international law, then under Japanese law the atomic bombing became a case of *massacre* that could not be legitimized by international law; under domestic law the crime automatically entailed the responsibility of its perpetrators. At this point, the issue became purely a matter of municipal law: was Japan itself to be held responsible for having illegally waived the claims of its citizens?

Here, I should like to point out that *in actual practice* the Court could have *evaded* the international issue and examined the case only from the point of view of Japanese law: had it decided that, even assuming the bombing was an international delict, the Japanese government had not violated the Constitution when it signed the Peace Treaty and waived its citizens' claims, the international legal issue would automatically have become irrelevant. The Court did in fact decide that the Treaty was not contrary to the Constitution. Japan had thereby waived all 'claims' that Japanese citizens might put forward *in accordance with Japanese law*. As the Court remarked, the right to claim damages for the bombing could only exist in *inter-state relations*; in other words, only the Japanese government could request payment of these damages from the United States. Under municipal law in Japan, the right to claim compensation did *not* belong to private citizens, because Japan recognized the principle of a foreign state's immunity from jurisdiction: the United States could not be sued by Shimoda and the other plaintiffs for damages due to the atomic bombs. Consequently, when Japan waived by treaty its citizens' 'claims' it had not renounced Shimoda's rights because these rights *did not exist*.

Shimoda's plea was set aside by the Court, which could have limited its decision to a rejection based on the reasons summarized above. Instead, to its great credit, *it decided to examine at length the international issue* of whether it had been lawful to launch the atomic bomb and, indeed, it devoted the main section of its judgement to its findings. In essence, the Court agreed with the plaintiffs: after a detailed examination of the rules of international law and the relevant facts, it declared that the United States had violated international law because it had ignored the ban on indiscriminate bombing of 'undefended cities', as well as the ban on weapons that cause superfluous suffering. Even though the Court's reasoning is not entirely watertight, nevertheless this is the only decision in which it is stated explicitly that the bombing of Hiroshima and Nagasaki was contrary to the fundamental precepts of international law.

It is worth adding that the Court, knowing full well that its judgement closed the door to any future claims for damages by the plaintiffs, wound up with words that are well worth quoting. After noting that Japanese law on medical treatment (and other matters) to be given to the victims of the bombs fell far short of their real needs, it said:

> The defendant state [Japan] caused many nationals to die, injured them, and drove them to a precarious life by the war which it opened on its own authority and responsibility. Also, the seriousness of the damage cannot compare a moment with that of the general calamity. Needless to say the defendant state should take sufficient relief measures in this light.
>
> That is, however, no longer the duty of the Court, but a duty which the diet or legislature or the cabinet or the executive must perform. Moreover, it is by such a procedure that relief measures can be taken not only by the parties to this suit, but also by the general sufferers of the atomic bombs: and there lies the *raison d'être* of the legislature and the administration. It cannot possibly be understood that the above is financially impossible in Japan, which has achieved a high degree of economic growth after the war. We cannot see this suit without regretting the political poverty [of Japan].

These are terribly severe words, a fair summing up to a splendid decision, in which the judges proved their independence *vis-à-vis* their own government – even though they had to bow to traditional imperatives, that is the rule on the exemption of foreign states from jurisdiction. They also demonstrated the role that a municipal court can play when it *takes a firm stance* on issues that induce governments to adopt diplomatic caution and respond by political fence-sitting.

Torture in Paraguay: the Filartiga case

Another decision worth examining at some length concerns the torture and killing of a young man from Paraguay by an officer of the same state: the famous *Filartiga* case.[6]

Paraguay is a small nation with no more than three million inhabitants and great poverty; for the last thirty years it has been ruled by the iron gauntlet of Stroessner, whose regime of terror has kept the country in a very backward state. The health service is equally behind the times and practically non-existent for those who cannot pay. In 1960 Dr Joel Filartiga decided to set up a hospital which he called the 'Clinic of Hope' (*el sanatorio la esperanza*) to tend the sick *campesinos* for nothing, or almost nothing, in the very poor area around the small town of Ybycuì, eighty miles away from Asunciòn. Soon, the hospital was offering relief to between 32,000 and 37,000 *campesinos*. Dr Filartiga was assisted by his wife and three daughters, whereas Joelito, his youngest child, gave a hand as a driver when he was not at school. The enormous cost of keeping the hospital going could hardly be covered by the tiny contribution from the patients' fees (who usually paid in kind, collecting firewood or offering the produce of their farms); to a large extent, money came from the sale of pictures from Dr Filartiga's collection, sold mostly in Mexico and the United States. Inevitably, in a country like Paraguay, the authorities' suspicions were aroused by so much generosity towards the poor: since he was making no money and only wanted to help the peasants, he must be a revolutionary. The government's doubts increased when it was discovered that Filartiga often went to the frontier town of Posadas, on the Argentinian border, to visit his mother. When a group of guerrillas, who had trained in Argentina, crossed the border at Posadas, the authorities immediately leapt to the conclusion that Filartiga had made a secret pact with them. In 1976, while the doctor was away from Asunciòn (at the Ybycuì hospital), a Paraguayan police inspector, Peña-Irala, had Joelito (who was seventeen) seized by a police squad and taken to police headquarters, where he was interrogated and tortured for information on the 'subversive activities' of his father. The whole episode was recorded on tape. Of course Joelito had nothing to confess and died a few hours later of heart failure caused by electric shocks. Taken aback by the turn of events, Peña-Irala and his subordinates decided to simulate a *crime passionnel* (feigning that the boy had been killed by another man who had discovered him in bed with his young wife). But the despicable subterfuge was soon revealed as a fake. The doctor managed to get hold of his son's battered body and had it exposed to public view before the funeral; he also distributed thousands of photographs of his son's mutilated remains both in Paraguay and abroad. A barrister he had nominated to start criminal proceedings against Peña-Irala was arrested and expelled from the Bar; later on, Paraguayan court rejected the Filartiga case; but it had now attracted world-wide attention. (A *campesino* told Filartiga: 'Doctor, how can you understand what has happened to you? You are too near to it all. But we understand. Your son was not killed because he was Filartiga's son, but because he was the son of a man who had helped us, the poor people.)' The case received a great deal of publicity in the United States. In 1977, after pressure from America, Stroessner decided to 'sack' Peña-Irala. In 1978, Peña-Irala went to the United States and, although he entered the country with a three-month visa, settled in Brooklyn. Meanwhile, Dr Filartiga's daughter, Dolly, had asked for political asylum and was living in Washington. Informed of the Paraguayan inspector's whereabouts, Dolly and her father decided to sue Peña-Irala before the Court of New York, to claim compensation for the torture of Joelito. The Immigration Office had Peña-Irala arrested, accusing him of having disobeyed the regulations on residence (he had overstayed the three months granted by his visa). Peña-Irala requested an order of deportation and this was granted. Fortunately, a judge at the District Court stayed the order so as to allow the trial against him to proceed.

The trial itself began in 1978 and, after various stages, it ended in 1983 with a victory for the Filartiga family. Unfortunately, in the meantime, the order suspending Peña-Irala's expulsion from the country had been quashed by the American courts and he had left the United States. The final decision (of 13 May 1983) by which Peña-Irala was sentenced to pay Joelito's father $200,000 and his sister $175,000 was never carried out because he was now safe in Paraguay.

Once again, however, what matters is that the judges gave a ruling not only on the question of torture, but also condemned Peña-Irala in unequivocal terms, thereby creating an extremely important precedent.

The problem facing the Filartiga lawyers and the New York judges was not an easy one. On the whole, the courts of one country do not emit a decision on crimes (or on the civil responsibility following from crimes) committed abroad, by foreigners against foreigners. In this case, a Paraguayan had tortured to death another Paraguayan in the territory of

Paraguay. No 'link' existed between the crime and the United States, where the trial was held. Usually, there must be some connection between the crime and the state where the criminal is to be tried. Either the victim, or the criminal, should be a national of the state in question, or else the crime should have been committed on the territory of that state. None of this was true in the *Filartiga* case. However, the doctor's lawyers managed to trace an old American procedural rule from an act passed in 1789, which had almost never been applied. The rule states that 'the district courts shall have jurisdiction of any civil action by an alien for a tort only, committed in violation of the law of nations or a treaty of the United States.' Thus, it remained to be proved that Peña-Irala had indeed violated international law. Since the United States has never ratified any treaty prohibiting torture, they also had to prove that torture is banned by a *customary* rule of international law. Although the *Filartiga* case was turned down by the District Court of New York, the family appealed and the Departments of Justice and of State decided to present in unison a memorandum to the Court as *amici curiae* (Carter was President at the time). This vitally important memorandum weighted the scales in favour of the Filartigas. The Court of Appeals accepted their plea and in 1980 sent the case back to the District Court which, in 1983, decided in their favour, as we have seen.[5]

Thus, both the Departments and the Court of Appeals decided that torture is covered by a *general rule of international law*, which prohibits it in any shape or form. The importance of these pronouncements is considerable. Yet, today, many jurists still doubt that such a rule exists; they point out that a number of states still practice it, albeit while denying they do so. From this these jurists infer that it is futile to speak of the existence of an international ban on torture. Nevertheless, both the Departments and the Court of Appeals gave their full support to the existence of such a rule, advancing solid, detailed and well-reasoned arguments as grounds for their opinion. It will be difficult, henceforth, to deny that states are obliged by law not to practice torture, even if they have never ratified a treaty on this subject.

The decision of the New York Court of Appeals is very important from another point of view. Peña-Irala had not acted as a private citizen when he arrested and tortured Joelito; he had acted as an agent for the state of Paraguay. This case raised the issue of the 'immunity of state agencies'. Indeed, the defendant stated before the Court of Appeals that 'if the conduct complained of is alleged to be the act of the Paraguayan government, the suit is barred by the Act of State doctrine.' At this point it is worth reminding readers who are not familiar with US law that since 1800 the American courts have always applied the 'doctrine' to which the defendant referred. This, to quote a famous decision of the Supreme Court in 1897 (*Underhill* v. *Hernandez*), goes as follows:

> Every sovereign state is bound to respect the independence of every other state, and the courts of one country will not sit in judgment on the acts of the government of another done within its own territory. Redress of grievances by reason of such acts must be obtained through the means open to be availed of by sovereign powers as between themselves.[7]

This 'doctrine' coincides in part with the rule on state immunity from jurisdiction, and in part it echoes the rule on the 'immunity of state agencies' which I mentioned at the beginning of this essay. Among other things it is based on the duty to respect the 'immunity' of individuals acting for foreign states. Peña-Irala had requested that his 'immunity' as an individual working for a government agency be recognized.

The Court of Appeals dealt somewhat summarily with the issue. First, it noted that the objection had not been advanced before the District Court and was not, therefore, among the points to be examined in appeal. It then added, 'in passing', the following remarks:

> We doubt whether action by a state official in violation of the Constitution and laws of the Republic of Paraguay, and wholly unratified by that nation's government, could properly be characterized as an act of state . . . Paraguay's renunciation of torture as a legitimate instrument of state policy, however, does not strip the tort of its character as an international law violation, if it in fact occurred under color of government authority.[8]

Both these remarks seem somewhat unclear and contradictory. On the one hand, the Court declares that Peña-Irala had not acted as a government agent when he committed the crime;

on the other, it states that, in any case, the crime violated international law (hence, it was to be attributed to a state).

Most probably, the Court had an intuitive perception of the correct solution, though it had expressed itself rather awkwardly. This is that torture, like genocide and other crimes against humanity, *even when it is committed by a state agent, does not exonerate the latter from individual responsibility*. In other words, torture should be considered on a par with *these other crimes against humanity*, and therefore international law does not allow any defence for those who practice it.

The Court's decision was interesting from a third point of view as well, in interpreting the 1789 procedural rule, which allowed the Court to assert its jurisdiction in the matter. When it was drafted, the rule was obviously intended to meet the needs that lay behind all the 'internationalistic' rules of the US Constitution: the need to grant the *federal* agencies the sole capacity for dealing with matters of foreign policy or for solving international issues, relieving the single *states* and their agencies of any say on these issues. As the Court itself stated, questions of international import 'are fraught with implications for the nation as a whole, and therefore should not be left to the potentially varying adjudications of the courts of the fifty states'. The wording of the statute and the relatively rare occasions on which it has been applied, prove that it was conceived mainly to deal with violations of international law committed by *US agencies against foreigners* and violations committed by *foreigners against other foreign individuals*. Of the two cases in which the US courts applied the statute to declare their competence, one, in 1795, concerned the actions of a US agency against some foreigners, while the other, in 1961, concerned relations between two Lebanese (one had forged the passport of a minor, declared by both to be their son, and this was considered by the court to be a violation of international law).

In the *Filartiga* case, the Court gave a much broader interpretation to the 1789 statute, asserting that it covered not only violations of international law by the *agencies* of a foreign state against foreign individuals, but also violations committed by a foreign agency against *nationals of the same state* as the agency. It is worth recording here that, in 1976, in a suit concerning the confiscation by the Nazi government of property belonging to a

German Jew, a US court, in application of that statute, held that 'violations of international law do not occur when the aggrieved parties are nationals of the acting state.'[9]

Thus, the New York Court gave an interpretation of the statute that overruled the traditional ones. By so doing, it acknowledged the need to mete out some form of punishment for grave violations of international law perpetrated by the agencies of a foreign state, overruling in this case the opposite requirements of state sovereignty. Had the Court respected the latter, who would have convicted Peña-Irala for his crimes? If the principle of sovereign immunity had been allowed to prevail, only another *state* could have forced Paraguay to answer for acts of torture. But what state, in a world where the idea of nationalism has such deep roots, would have insisted that Paraguay respect an international rule created to protect the human rights of Paraguayans? The New York Court circumnavigated with skill the enormous obstacles that the 'old pattern' of the world community had created, and acted with great wisdom when it applied the criteria that underpin the 'new' international law – which, to date, exists only as a set of 'rules'. If Peña-Irala's hurried return to Paraguay, to which the US courts gave their consent, prevented the Filartigas from obtaining compensation, this must not upset us. They did not want money, but an authoritative judgement 'condemning' the inspector's crimes.

Before leaving this famous 'affair', I should like to underscore one point that makes it quite unique and helps to explain the revolutionary power of the Court's decision. In this suit the Administration – which in so many other cases has done its best to obstruct the work of municipal courts – helped the Court and even urged it to go in the right direction, not only by presenting a memorandum as *amicus curiae*, but also by offering it the legal 'key' and logical reasons for a convincing and just decision. This happy instance of co-operation between the Judiciary and the Executive, an exceptional circumstance that can only be explained by the favourable climate towards the human rights issue created by President Carter, made this *volte face* possible. Thanks to this judgement, and in spite of subsequent judicial set-backs, human values trodden underfoot by authoritarian governments can now be defended in foreign courts.

Political assassination in foreign lands: the Letelier case

Let us now turn to another case, no less important than the first, heard by the District Court of the District of Columbia in 1980. After the fall of President Allende in 1973, many political figures who had fought on his side were forced to flee abroad. One of these, Orlando Letelier, had been Foreign Minister and then Ambassador for Chile to the United States. When Pinochet came to power, he was granted political asylum in the United States, where he did research for the Institute for Policy Studies in Washington. One day in 1976, Letelier was driving away from the Institute with Mrs Moffit (the wife of one of the Institute's members) when a bomb, planted at night under the car, exploded and killed them both. The FBI soon traced the crime to an American citizen, M. V. Townley, who had been paid to plant the bomb by the Chilean secret service. After his arrest, Townley decided to help inquiries in the hope of a reduced sentence and named all the other members of the group of assassins. His account led to the arrest of three of the eight Chilean accomplices and a request for the extradition of the remaining five, which was ignored by Chile. Townley and the other three were tried and sentenced to varying terms of imprisonment.

Contemporaneously with these criminal proceedings, the families of the two victims brought a civil suit against the Republic of Chile, its intelligence service (the Centro Nacional de Inteligencia, CNI) and the individual CNI agents involved in the assassination of Letelier and Mrs Moffit. The aim of this second trial was to obtain compensation.

When the Chilean government was summonsed to appear before the District Court of the District of Columbia, it objected that the Court did not have jurisdiction over the matter for two reasons. First, Chile was exempt from jurisdiction by virtue of the US Foreign Sovereign Immunities Act of 1976. On this point Chile suggested that, even admitting it was responsible for the assassinations – and this it denied – US law only allowed foreign states to be sued for private torts (such as motor car accidents), and never for acts, such as political assassination, that are of a 'public, governmental character'.

Second, the Chilean government observed that, even admitting it was implicated in the affair, the acts of which it stood accused (the decision to kill Letelier, the plans for his assassination, etc.) were of a 'public nature', carried out in Chile, not in the United States; hence the Court should have applied the Act of State doctrine which covers acts performed *abroad* by a foreign government. This was further proof that the US Court had no jurisdiction over the case at hand.

The Court rejected both arguments in its decision of 11 March 1980. Later, in another judgement of 5 November 1980, it sentenced the Chilean government by default to pay the compensation requested by the two families.[10]

The case was not an easy one. If the Court had decided to follow the general trend of municipal courts and generally accepted international practice, it would have decided it did lack jurisdiction and it would have been up to the *two governments* to settle the dispute via the appropriate diplomatic channels. However, the Court preferred to break new ground and assert the right of municipal judges to pronounce upon the acts of foreign governments. Its argument hinged upon the 1976 Foreign Sovereign Immunities Act, to which it gave an extremely broad interpretation.

First, the Court examined the part of the Act on which Chile had based its objections (section 1605(a) paragraph 5). Under this section a foreign state cannot be exempt from the jurisdiction of US courts in suits claiming compensation for damages caused in the United States by the unlawful acts of that state, or of one of its officials. According to the Court, neither the wording nor the preparatory work on the Act showed that it distinguished between 'private' and 'public' acts. Consequently, it was useless to argue that, since the action was of a 'public' nature, the Chilean government was immune from the jurisdiction of US courts. Then the Court advanced another argument, based on another provision of US law, one which Chile had not invoked. Subparagraph A of the section quoted above allows for one exception: American courts do not have jurisdiction over 'any claim based upon the exercise or performance or the failure to exercise or perform a discretionary function, regardless of whether the discretion was abused'.

Quite rightly, the Court wondered whether the political assassination of Letelier and the decision to commit the crime would be considered one of the Chilean government's 'discretionary acts'. One is tempted to ask what is more 'discretionary' than a government's decision to have a political opponent killed in a foreign country. The Court took the opposite view. When is an act 'discretionary'? it asked. According to the Supreme Court of the United States, an act is 'discretionary' when 'there is room for policy judgement and decision'. This being so, in the District Court's view, one cannot qualify as 'discretionary' the decision to commit, or have others commit, an illegal act: 'Whatever policy options may exist for a foreign country, it has no "discretion" to perpetrate conduct designed to result in the assassination of an individual or individuals, action that is clearly contrary to the precepts of humanity as recognized in both national and international law'.

The Court reasoned with boldness and subtlety when it interpreted the Act as meaning that an action is discretionary only if it is *legal*; any unlawful act – defined by the Court as *contrary to the 'precepts of humanity'* – is no longer 'discretionary' because it is merely illegal: by acting unlawfully, Chile had renounced the protective armour of immunity.

It is interesting to reflect on the difference between this reasoning and the arguments advanced in 1840 by the British government, and accepted by the government of the United States, in the *McLeod* case. Though the two suits referred to different rules (one to the immunity of state agencies, the other to immunity from jurisdiction), the 'liberal' and 'internationalist' views expressed in 1980 are eons away from the nationalist ones that, in 1840, were dictated by the principle of sovereignty and the need to maintain a 'dialogue between governments'.

However, the Court's interpretation of the 1976 Act was not sufficient to conclude the suit; the other arguments advanced by Chile and based on the Act of State doctrine had yet to be examined. This was a particularly strong point because it was supported by the whole of American case-law. Nevertheless, the Court was in no way discouraged: it asserted the 'doctrine' was inapplicable to the suit. The alleged actions of the Chilean state agency, even though they had indeed been decided, planned and set in motion on Chilean soil, had 'resulted in tortious injury in this country'. At first sight, this statement might seem to be rather questionable, since all the suits in which the doctrine had been invoked previously in the United States had dealt with the damaging *consequences* produced there by illegal acts committed abroad. However, in this particular case, the determining factor was that, although the crime had been decided and planned in Chile, it had been actually *carried out* in the United States. The District Court supported its view with yet another reason. It observed that, should its argument be refuted, the main aim of the 1976 Act would have been without effect: what had been kicked out by the front door, would be let in by the back door. In other words, if the Chilean objection were accepted, the exemption from jurisdiction denied by the Act would have to be accepted because of the Act of State doctrine, thus thwarting the very reasons for which the Foreign Sovereignty Immunities Act had been passed.

Taken as a whole, I feel the District Court's reasoning is convincing. In any case, the Court was right in preventing the old Act of State doctrine from being used as shield by foreign states that behave in a manner contrary to the elementary rules of civilized society.

Torture and racial persecution for economic gain: the Siderman case

Like the others we have examined, the Siderman case was heard by an American court: the District Court of California.[11]

The Sidermans are an Argentinian family of Jewish origin who lived in Tucumàn in a northern province of Argentina. They were extremely rich, owning a very large hacienda, as well as one of the largest modern hotels in the north of Argentina (for they owned all the shares in the company, Inosa, which ran the hotel).

On 24 March 1976, the night of the *golpe* when Maria Estela Peròn was overthrown and a military dictatorship took over the country's government, the Sidermans were woken by armed men with machine-guns who roughed up various members of the family, blindfolded José Siderman and dragged him off with them. The man was 65 at the time. For seven long days he was kept a prisoner, blindfolded throughout, maltreated, tortured and insulted for being a Jew. Before he was set free on the outskirts of the town, his captors warned him to leave the country, with all his family, if he wished to escape with his life. Various clues made it clear that he had been captured by agents of General Bussi, the military commander of Tucumàn. Terrified, the Sidermans sold off part of their land, named an agent to run the Inosa company, and escaped to the United States. After their escape, General Bussi and his acolyte, Captain Abas, had all the documents concerning the Sidermans' land faked or altered so that it appeared that they owned 57 and not 57,000 hectares. This was done to make it easier for the two men to gain possession of the land, bit by bit. Then they had the Inosa company put into receivership, after having the Sidermans' accountant and agent imprisoned and killed. From then on they began to run the company themselves and to sell its assets, pocketing all the profits. From the United States the Sidermans brought a suit in the Argentinian courts against the receivership of their company and, after various trials, they won their case. However, the court order was never enforced. All this confirms that José's torture was intended as a form of racial persecution, designed to provoke the Sidermans' flight from Argentina so that the perpetrators of the torture could lay hands on the family property.

The Siderman affair produced echoes in Italy, too. In 1981 José Siderman came to Italy to visit some friends, but he was arrested (on a request for extradition by Argentina) for having faked his passport before leaving Argentina. On 19 December 1981, the Tribunal of Brescia decided the Argentinian accusations were baseless and the request for Siderman's extradition was intended to allow the government to submit him to forms of duress that are contrary to international law. This episode clearly revealed once again the real intentions of the Argentinian government *vis-à-vis* the Siderman family.

Feeling weary of all this persecution and realizing that the Argentinian courts would never give them redress, the Sidermans turned to the US courts. They brought a suit against the Republic of Argentina and the province of Tucumàn claiming damages for José's torture and the persecution of the Siderman family for racial reasons, as well as for having illegally seized their land and assets.

The Republic of Argentina was informed of the suit via the usual diplomatic channels. In a letter of 16 February 1983, it voiced strong objections because

> As a sovereign state it enjoys immunity of jurisdiction regarding foreign courts on [sic] all acts of authority exercised according to its rights and aimed to ensure the general administration of the country and its function as a government.[12]

The plaintiffs pointed out that the Republic had already renounced this exemption in various ways. Besides, Argentina had ratified various treaties on human rights, thus it had implicitly relinquished the right to claim exemption from jurisdiction for acts that violate those rights. The plaintiffs adduced other reasons, but two of these were outstanding. First, US courts had jurisdiction in the matter by virtue of the 1976 Foreign Sovereign Immunities Act (which grants American courts the right to decide on the acts of foreign state agencies that expropriate assets in violation of international law). Second, American courts could adjudicate the matter because of the 1789 Act, quoted in the Filartiga case: here, too, a foreigner claimed damages for a wrongful international act and, under US law, this entailed the responsibility of the state that committed the tort.

On 28 September 1984, the District Court of California gave a rather disappointing verdict: it was too terse and based on too few arguments. Nevertheless, on the whole the Court decided in favour of the Siderman family. The judges held they had no jurisdiction over the illegal expropriation of the family's property by the Argentinian authorities, because it was 'covered' by the Act of State doctrine. On the other hand, the judges did feel they had jurisdiction on the *torture charge*. Although it did not advance any argument to justify its view, the Court condemned the Republic of Argentina and the province of Tucumàn to pay the sum they deemed appropriate to José Siderman and Lea, his wife.

To sum up

Let me now try to draw to a close this rather long essay and gather up the general ideas underlying the various remarks I have made along the way.

The first and most obvious point is that all the judgements quoted here were decided by *Western* courts (obviously, from the political point of view, Japan belongs to the Western group of states). This is no accident. Western democracies allow their judges greater leeway in breaking new ground and adopting stances that are unwelcome to the Executive and in helping international law to widen its horizons by putting forward new interpretations. Furthermore, it is no accident that most of these cases were heard in the United States. It is well known that there are American judges and lawyers with strong liberal tendencies and that a lively debate on matters of substantive justice is carried on in the United States; besides, in America the weight of public opinion has always been considerable. To all these reasons another should be added: a nation as strong as the United States can allow its courts to 'condemn' less powerful countries such as Paraguay, Chile or Argentina. The balance of power between these countries is such that it is unlikely the latter would ever protest effectively against the decisions of the US courts, or allow their own courts, by way of 'retaliation', to emit similar verdicts against the United States. These reflections may dampen our enthusiasm and make it unlikely that those 'front-line' judges will see the early flowering of the new plant whose seed they have sown. Furthermore, even in the United States, other courts have repeatedly taken far less bold decisions.[13]

This second remark leads me to a theme I touched on earlier. The decisions examined in this essay all show the same trend: judges feel less and less bound to avoid *international issues traditionally considered the exclusive preserve of the executive*. It is no coincidence that the slow corrosion of executive power has come about in the very area in which the whole international community has proved to be readier to make concessions. Indeed, on closer examination, the two rules intended to protect state governments ('immunity from jurisdiction' and 'immunity of state agencies'), frequently pruned or circumvented by modern courts, had already been undermined in earlier times. Initially states were granted 'full' immunity from jurisdiction, but after the Second World War this was generally accepted as 'restricted' immunity, that is immunity only for 'public' or 'governmental' activities and not for commercial ones. Besides, the rule on immunity for state agencies, from its very inception, excluded war crimes (war criminals could be impleaded and condemned even when they had acted on behalf of state agencies) and was further reduced after the Second World War by the exclusion of crimes against peace and crimes against humanity. Whereas the reasons for limiting exemption from jurisdiction were of a historical and economic nature (since states engaged more and more often in economic and commercial activities, their exemption from the jurisdiction of local domestic courts for private activities was clearly unjust and obsolete), the gradual 'restriction' of the rule on 'immunity of agencies' was mainly the result of a trend towards humanitarian values after 1945.

The decisions described in these pages mark the ulterior erosion of these two rules; they respond to obvious ethical and political imperatives. It would be contrary to the elementary principles of justice to witness the use of banned weapons, torture, political persecution or odious forms of discrimination in other states or by other states without doing anything about it, and deny the individual the right to go to law in a democratic country when a minimum of 'contact' exists between that country and the people involved in these grave violations.

Seen in this light, the new trend towards an ever increasing interference of domestic courts in international affairs is certainly a step in the right direction, even though it will undoubtedly cause friction between states. (The government impleaded and condemned by the local foreign court might consider this interference an 'unfriendly act' and retaliate.) In point of fact the case-law I have just put before the reader reflects the international community's new tendency to make *respect for human dignity* prevail over the need to safeguard *state sovereignty* and maintain *peaceful relations* among sovereign states. Let me add that this case-law should not vex governments excessively since it is concerned almost exclusively with the *civil* responsibilities of foreign states and their agencies. It is no accident that domestic courts rarely decide on the *criminal* implications of the alleged unlawful acts of foreign states. Should this occur, the 'interference' of the courts would be more far-reaching and the outcome more unpredictable.

The decisions I have been discussing have two other important aspects. They *help to define* the international rules that cover extremely sensitive areas (such as torture, or the lawfulness of using certain weapons in warfare); they also clarify the rules on the exemption of foreign states from jurisdiction and the 'immunity of agencies'. Thus, domestic courts have contributed significantly to the development and clarification of international precepts that are often woolly or imprecise. However, in their interpretation of these rules, the courts have done more: as local blacksmiths they have tempered these rules in the fire of real cases. In other words, they have *ensured* that these international rules be respected by taking over the function of governments (which, all too often, seem unmoved by grave violations) and *substituting themselves* for the international supervisory mechanisms that either do not exist at all or have proved to be extremely ineffectual.

Notes

Introduction

1 G. De Staël, *De l'Allemagne* (Garnier-Flammarion, Paris, 1968) vol. II, p. 128.

2 A. Camus, 'Vers le dialogue,' *Actuelles I* (1944–8), in A. Camus, *Essais* (La Pléiade, Gallimard, Paris, 1965), p. 352 ('Et désormais le seul honneur sera de tenir obstinément ce formidable pari qui décidera enfin si les paroles sont plus fortes que les balles').

3 W. Churchill, *The Second World War*, vol. VI, *Triumph and Tragedy* (Cassel, London, 1954), p. 554.

4 B. V. A. Röling, *International Law in an Expanded World* (Djambatan N.V., Amsterdam 1960), p. 2.

5 D. Acheson, 'Remarks', in *Proceedings of the American Society of International Law* (57th Annual Meeting), 1963, p. 14.

6 I. Kant, *Zum ewigen Frieden. Ein philosophischer Entwurf* in *Politische Schriften*, ed. O. H. von der Gablentz (Westdeutscher Verlag, Köln-Opladen, 1965), p. 117.

7 The German document is a memorandum sent on 9 August 1915 by the German ambassador to Turkey to the Turkish Ministry of foreign affairs. It is appended to the dispatch of 8 October 1915 of the German ambassador to the USA to the Secretary of State Lansing: see *Papers Relating to the Foreign Relations of the US, 1915, Supplement: The World War* (US Government Printing Office, Washington, 1928), p. 990.

8 J. L. Brierly, 'Sanctions' (1931), in *The Basis of Obligation in International Law*, (Oxford University Press, Oxford, 1958), p. 203.

1 Hiroshima, Nagasaki and the Imperatives of the International Community

1 J. A. Siemes, 'Hiroshima – August 6, 1945 . . .', *Bulletin of the Atomic Scientists* 1.11 (15 May 1946) p. 5.

2 Ibid., p. 4.

3 For the complete text of the telegram see A. Durand, *Histoire du*

Comité international de la Croix-Rouge. De Sarajevo à Hiroshima (Institut Henry-Dunan, Genève, 1978), p. 552.

4 Siemes, 'Hiroshima' pp. 5–6.

5 The various eyewitness accounts of the survivors in Hiroshima and Nagasaki that I quote in my essay can be found in *Plus jamais. Le combat pour la paix des survivants d'Hiroshima* (Flammarion, Paris, 1982), pp. 151–248. See also *Time Magazine*, 29 July 1985, p. 22ff.

6 J. Hersey, *Hiroshima* (Penguin, London, 1966), p. 105.

7 The Portuguese declaration can be found, in the French original, in *Nouveau Recueil Général des Traités – Continuation du Grand Recueil de G. Fr. Martens*, ed. C. Samwer and J. Hopf, vol. 18 (Göttingen, 1873), p. 464.

8 For the various official statements on prohibited weapons, see A. Cassese, 'Weapons causing unnecessary suffering: are they prohibited?' *Rivista di diritto internazionale* 58 (1975), p. 12 ff; and 'The prohibition of indiscriminate means of warfare', *Declarations on Principles. A Quest for Universal Peace*, ed. R. J. Akkerman, P. J. Van Krieken and C. O. Pannenborg (Sijthoff, Leyden, 1977), p. 171ff.

9 Churchill's declaration is reported in *Keesing's Contemporary Archives*, 1943–1946, p. 6536–7.

10 The military manual of the Federal Republic of Germany is called *Kriegsvölkerrecht. Allgemeine Bestimmungen des Kriegführungsrechts und Landkriegsrecht* (ZDv 15/10, March 1961), para. 90.

11 For Truman's declarations see *Public Papers of the Presidents of the US: Harry S. Truman – Containing the Public Messages, Speeches and Statements of the President, April 12 to December 31, 1946* (Washington, 1961), pp. 197ff; 212, 362, 379, 435. See also Harry S. Truman, *Memoirs, I, Year of Decisions* (Doubleday, Garden City, NY, 1955), pp. 10–11, 85–87, 208–211, 416ff, 523ff.

12 Henry L. Stimson, 'The decisions to use the atomic bomb, *Harper's Magazine* 194.1161 (February 1947), pp. 97–107. See also H. L. Stimson and McGeorge Bundy, *On Active Service in Peace and War* (Harper, New York, 1947), pp. 621–4.

13 W. Churchill, in *Keesing's Contemporary Archives*, 18–25 August 1945, p. 7383; and *The Second World War*, p. 545ff.

14 The views of James F. Byrnes are reported by L. Szilard, *His Version of the Facts, Selected Recollections and Correspondence*, ed. S. R. Weart and G. Weiss Szilard (MIT Press, Cambridge Mass., 1978), p. 89. The view whereby the atomic bomb was used primarily for the purpose of somewhat influencing the USSR was put forward by the American historian G. Alperowitz in *Atomic Diplomacy: Hiroshima and Potsdam* (Praeger, New York, 1956). It has been criticized by various other historians: see for instance B. B. Bernstein ed., *The*

Atomic Bomb: the Critical Issues (Basic Books, Boston, 1976), pp. 69–71; McGeorge Bundy, 'The unimpressive record of atomic diplomacy', in G. Prins ed., *The Choice: Nuclear Weapons v. Security* (Chatto and Windus, London, 1984), p. 44.

15 See *Plus jamais*, p. 178.

16 Henry L. Stimson, 'The decisions to use the atomic bomb', p. 104. In his memoirs W. A. Harriman points out that Stimson's proposal was attacked by Byrnes before Truman criticized it. See W. A. Harriman and E. Abel, *Special Envoy to Churchill and Stalin 1941–1946* (Hutchinson, London, 1976), p. 492.

17 B. V. A. Röling, 'The significance of the laws of war', in A. Cassese ed, *Current Problems of International Law* (Giuffré, Milano, 1975), pp. 143–4.

18 The Japanese diplomat who participated in the mission to Moscow is professor Tsuru. His opinion, expressed in a personal letter to J. Robinson, is reported in Robinson, 'The arms race', in *The Tanner Lectures on Human Values*, vol. 3 (University of Utah Press, Utah, 1982), p. 265.

19 Robert J. C. Butow, *Japan's Decision to Surrender* (Stanford University Press, Stanford, 1954), pp. 112 n.2; 130; 132; 142ff; 231.

20 For the text of the Japanese protest see *The Japanese Annual of International Law* 8 (1964), pp. 251–2.

21 For the new Japanese stand, see *The Japanese Annual of International Law*, p. 226.

22 For the Franck report see *Bulletin of the Atomic Scientists* 1.10 (1st May 1946), p. 2ff.

23 Stimson, 'The decision to use the atomic bomb', pp. 100–1.

24 L. Szilard, 'His version of the facts'. p. 95.

25 L. Szilard, ibid. p. 90.

26 The text of the petition is reproduced in M. Grodzins and E. Rabinowitch eds, *The Atomic Age: Scientists in National and World Affairs (Articles from the 'Bulletin of the Atomic Scientists' 1945–1962)*, (Basic Books, New York, 1963), pp. 28–9.

27 S. Freud, 'Das Unbehagen in der Kultur', in *Das Unbewusste – Schriften zur Psychoanalyse*, ed. A. Mitscherlich, (S. Fischer Verlag, Frankfurt am Main, 1960), p. 366.

2   Why States Use Force with Impunity: The 'Black Holes' of International Law

1 For a general survey of international practice on the use of force as well as of the attitude of states on this subject, see A. Cassese, *International Law in a Divided World* (Oxford University Press, Oxford, 1986), pp. 215–50. See also A. Cassese ed., *The Current*

Legal Regulation of the Use of Force (M. Nijhoff, Dordrecht, 1986), especially pp. 505–23.

3 Is the First Use of Nuclear Weapons Prohibited?

1 For the various US statements, see E. C. McDowell ed., *Digest of United States Practice in International Law 1975* (Washington, DC, Department of State Printing House, 1976), pp. 798–801. Reference to the 'right' of Western countries to use nuclear weapons in Korea, besides Europe, is made by McGeorge Bundy, 'The unimpressive record of atomic diplomacy', in G. Prins ed., *The Choice: Nuclear Weapons v. Security* (Chatto and Windus, London, 1984), p. 53.

2 V. R. Pipes, 'Why the Soviet Union thinks that it could fight and win a nuclear war', *Commentary* (July 1977), p. 22. Pipes's arguments have been criticized by A. S. Collins, 'Current NATO strategy: a recipe for disaster', in G. Prins ed., *The Choice*, p. 38.

3 V. M. Mandelbaum, *The Nuclear Future* (Cornell University Press, London, 1983), p. 72.

4 G. Barile, *Lezioni di diritto internazionale* (Cedam, Padova, 1977, pp. 50–1; 2nd ed, 1983, pp. 81–2).

5 See Organisation mondiale de la Santé, XXXVIème Assemblée, *Effets de la guerre nucléaire sur la santé et les services de santé*, 24 mars 1983, doc. A 36/12.

6 On the neutron bomb see H. Meyrowitz, "Problèmes juridiques relatifs à l'arme à neutrons', *Annuaire français de droit international* 27 (1981), p. 87ff. Very critical remarks are made by the Soviet author T. Dmitrichev 'The neutron weapon in the US aggressive strategy', *International Affairs* 8 (Moscow) (1984), pp. 96–103.

7 E. Korowin, 'The A-weapons *vs.* international law', *International Affairs* (Moscow) (1955), pp. 48–55.

8 For the USA see *Rules of Naval Warfare* (1955), para. 613; *Army Field Manual of Land Warfare* (1956), para. 35; Department of the Air Force, *International Law. The Conduct of Armed Conflict and Air Operations*, AF Pamphlet 110–31 (1976), para. 6/5. For the UK see: The War Office, *The War on Land* (1958), para. 107, note 1*b*; Ministry of Defence, *The Law of Armed Conflict* (1981), section 5, para. 2.

9 For the 1961 debates in the United Nations, see UN docs A/C.1/SR. 1181–94 (debates in the First Commission of the General Assembly) and A/PV.1063 (debates in the plenary).

10 For the 1972 debates see the following UN docs: *General Assembly Official Records*, XXVIIth Session, 2078th, 2084th and 2093rd plenary meetings. The GA adopted resolution 2936 (XXVII) of 29 November 1972.

11 The 1972 statement of the Chinese delegate can be found in *General Assembly Official Records*, XXVIIth Session, 2051st Plenary Meeting, para. 168. See also the following UN docs: A/SPC/SR.876 p. 7; A/SPC/SR.903, p. 12. See also the statement made on 6 August 1981 in the Committee on Disarmament: CD/207, p. 3. It would seem that the statement made on 11 June 1982 by the Chinese delegate to the Special Session of the General Assembly on Disarmament bears witness to the Chinese 'turning-point'. He stated among other things that, 'In point of fact, the Chinese Government has long since repeatedly pledged to the world that at no time and under no circumstances will China be the first to use nuclear weapons and that it undertakes unconditionally not to use weapons against non-nuclear states' (the text is taken from *China and the World*, Bejing, 1983, p. 16). Surprisingly, no mention of such a pledge was made on 13 February 1986 in the statement of the Chinese delegate to the Geneva Conference on Disarmament; see *Statement by Ambassador Quian Jiadong, head of the Chinese delegation, at the Plenary Meeting of the Conference on Disarmament*, Geneva, February 1986, p. 4. (Amb. Quian Jiadong simply stated that 'All nuclear states, the two big nuclear powers, the US and USSR in particular, should undertake not to be the first to use nuclear weapons in any circumstances and should unconditionally undertake not to use or threaten to use nuclear weapons against non-nuclear states or nuclear-free zones. Proceeding on such a basis, an international convention prohibiting the use of nuclear weapons should be concluded, with the participation of all nuclear states.')

12 For the debate on GA resolution 33/71 B of 14 December 1978, see UN Docs A/C.1/33/PV.7, 12, 14, 15, 18, 45 and 51. The Soviet statement is in A/C.1/33/PV. 51, pp. 53–5.

13 The Declaration by Gromyko is in UN ·loc. A/S–12/PV.12, pp. 22–3/25.

14 See I. Blishchenko, 'A guarantee of international security', *International Affairs* (Moscow) (February 1983), pp. 86–8.

15 See the statements made by the Soviet delegate at Geneva in 1975: *Official Records of the 1974–77 Geneva Conference on Humanitarian Law of Armed Conflict*, CDDH/IV/SR.19, para. 17. See also CDDH/SR.12, in *Official Records*, vol. 5, p. 121.

4 Negotiation Versus Force: The *Achille Lauro* Imbroglio

1 This, and the following quotations, are taken from Prime Minister Craxi's statement to the Chamber of Deputies, of 17 October 1985 (typewritten text distributed by the presidency of the Council of Ministers, 17 October 1985, pp. 26–7).

2 See Craxi's statement quoted at n.1, pp. 20–1.
3 UN doc. S/PV.2619, p. 17.
4 See the statement made on 10 October 1985 by the Principal Deputy Press Secretary, in *International Legal Materials*, vol. 24 (1985) pp. 1513–14.
5 See the note issued by the presidency of the Council of Ministers on 4 October 1986, pp. 2–6 (typewritten text).
6 See UN doc. S/PV. 2622, pp. 39/40–1.
7 See UN doc. S/17554.

5 Sabra and Shatila

1 See *International Legal Materials* 22 (1983), p. 473ff.
2 The text of this law is published in *Israel Law Review* 6 (1971), p. 410ff. For a comment on the law see P. Elman, 'The Commissions of Inquiry Law', ibid., p. 398ff.
3 The McBride report is called *Israel in Lebanon. Report of the International Commission to Inquire into Reported Violations of International Law by Israel during the Invasion of the Lebanon*, Ithaca Press, London, 1983.
4 Cf. International Committee of the Red Cross, *Draft Additional Protocols to the Geneva Conventions of August 12, 1949. Commentary*, Geneva, October 1973, p. 80.
5 See GA resolution 37/123D of 16 December 1982.
6 See UN docs A/37/PV.108, pp. 33–101.
7 For the text of the judgement in the *Yamashita* case see L. Friedman ed., *The Law of War. A Documentary History* vol. 2 (Random, New York, 1972), pp. 1596ff.
8 *The Law of War on Land* (The War Office, London, 1958, pp. 176–9 (paras 627–35).
9 *The Law of Land Warfare*, Department of the Army Field Manual, FM 27–10 July 1956, pp. 178–80 (paras 501–4); *International Law. The Conduct of Armed Conflict and Air Operations* (Washington, DC, 1976), pp. 15/2 (para. *d–e*).
10 *The Laws of War* (in Hebrew), Code of Military Laws, 17–2, 1963, Chapter 2, para. 9.
11 T. Hobbes, *Leviathan*, ed. C. B. Macpherson (Penguin Books, London 1983), p. 223.

6 Crime without punishment: the Captain Astiz affair

1 S. Satta, *Il giorno del guidizio*, 2nd edn. (Adelphi, Milano, 1979), p. 147.

2 A detailed account of Astiz's actions is given by M. A. Meyer, 'Liability of prisoners of war for offences committed prior to capture', *International and Comparative Law Quarterly* 32 (1983), pp. 948, 954. See also *Keesing's Contemporary Archives*, 1982, pp. 31717, 31537; 1984, p. 33090. See also *Revue générale de droit international public* 86 (1982), pp. 761ff.

3 For the official British stand, and references to the action of the ICRC, see Meyer, 'Liability of prisoners of war', pp. 955ff.

4 A contrary view is taken by Meyer, ibid., pp. 962–72.

5 The text of the Italian judgement in the *Wagener* case is reprinted in A. Cassese, *Diritto internazionale bellico moderno – Testi e documenti* (Libreria scientifica G. Pellegrini, Pisa, 1973), pp. 545ff. The passages quoted above are at pp. 573–4 and 580–1, respectively.

6 For the text of the decision on the *Eichmann* case, see *International Law Reports*, vol. 36 (Butterworths, London, 1968), pp. 277ff. The passage quoted is at p. 296.

7 Ibid., p. 298.

7 Klaus Barbie: The Exemplary Life of an Executioner

1 Madame Deletraz, a Frenchwoman working for the SS who secretly passed on information to the Maquis, learnt that the Gestapo knew all about the meeting and were about to arrest all those who took part. She rushed to warn the partisans, but her message was transmitted too late. Playing for time – she had been told by Barbie to follow the traitor who was to show the Gestapo where the meeting was being held – she returned with the SS and deliberately pretended to lose her way, thereby wasting an hour. She had hoped that the Resistance leaders would, meanwhile, have had time to get away. What she did not know was that many leaders (including Jean Moulin) arrived very late at the villa Caluire! (See H. Noguères, *La verité aura le dernier mot* (Seuil, Paris, 1985), pp. 59–62).

2 For the text of the letter of the Paris inquiring magistrate, see the documentary annex to L. De Hoyos, *Barbie* (Editions R. Laffont, Paris, 1984), p. 309.

3 Cf. L. De Hoyos, *Barbie*, p. 169.

4 On the life of Barbie see among other things: L. De Hoyes, *Barbie*; T. Bower, *Klaus Barbie, itineraire d'un bourreau ordinaire* Editions Calman-Lévy, Paris, 1984); E. Paris, *L'affaire Barbie, analyse d'un mal francais* (Editions Ramsay, Paris, 1985); E. Dabringhaus, *L'agent américain Klaus Barbie* (Editions Pygmalion, Paris, 1986); G. Morel, *Barbie – Pour mémoire* (Editions FNDIRP, Paris, 1986).

5 Cardinal Sforza Pallavicino's statement is quoted by F. De Sanctis, *Storia della letteratura italiana*, vol. 2 (Fratelli Treves editore, Milano,

1917), p. 225.

6 P. Levi, *Se questo è un uomo* (Einaudi, Torino, (1986), p. 244 (the three historians I mention in the text are quoted by Levi).

7 For the British stand, see the documents published in the excellent collection, *The American Road to Nuremberg: the Documentary Record, 1944–1945*, ed. B. F. Smith (Hoover Institution Press, Stanford, 1982), pp. 31–3, 155–7.

8 On this point, see the documents collected in B. F. Smith, ibid., pp. 30–1, 33–7, 40–1, 130, 158–9.

9 Cf. H. Arendt, *Eichmann in Jerusalem: a Report on the Banality of Evil* (Penguin Books, Harmondsworth 1976), pp. 269–271.

10 On the Calley trial see R. A. Falk, 'Son My: war crimes and individual responsibility', *Toledo Law Review* (Fall–Winter, 1971), p. 21ff.

11 See T. Bower, *Klaus Barbie*, pp. 19–20.

12 *L'Express*, 7 February 1983.

13 Cf E. Paris, *L'affaire Barbie*, pp. 30, 259.

14 *Le Nouvel Observateur*, 11 February 1983.

15 Cf. E. Paris, *l'affaire Barbie*, p. 33.

16 Cf. E. Paris, ibid., p. 167.

17 For the text of the documents, see B. F. Smith, *The American Road*, pp. 33–7.

18 See the various documents published by B. F. Smith, ibid., pp. 33–7, 98–105, 144, 158–72, 209–12.

19 Article 6 provides that the Tribunal established by the Agreement for the prosecution and punishment of the major war criminals of the European Axis

> shall have the power to try and punish persons who, acting in the interests of the European Axis countries, whether as individuals or as members of organisations, committed any of the following crimes:
>
> (a) Crimes against Peace: namely, planning, preparation, initiation or waging of a war of aggression, or a war in violation of international treaties, agreements or assurances, or participation in a common plan or conspiracy for the accomplishment of any of the foregoing;
>
> (b) War Crimes: namely, violations of the laws or customs of war. Such violations shall include, but not be limited to, murder, ill-treatment or deportation to slave labour or for any other purpose of civilian population of or in occupied territory, murder or ill-treatment of prisoners of war or persons on the seas, killing of hostages, plunder of public or private property, wanton destruction of cities, towns or villages, or devastation not justified by military necessity;
>
> (c) Crimes against Humanity: namely, murder, extermination,

enslavement, deportation, and other inhumane acts committed against any civilian population, before or during the war; or persecutions on political, racial, or religious grounds in execution of or in connection with any crime within the jurisdiction of the Tribunal, whether or not in violation of the domestic law of the country where perpetrated.

20 For the complete text of this document, see B. F. Smith, *The American Road*, p. 212.

21 See *Trial of the Major War Criminals before the International Military Tribunal*, vol. 1 (Nuremberg, 1947), p. 219.

22 The judgment is still unpublished. For a summary, see J.-M. Théolleyre, 'K. Barbie devra répondre des déportations de juifs et de celles des résistants déportés par la suite', *Le Monde*, 11 July 1986.

23 See p. 20 of the typewritten text of the judgement. Italics are mine.

24 See p. 42 of the typewritten report of Counsellor Le Gunehec.

25 On Jacques Vergès, see L. De Hoyes, *Barbie*, pp. 272–7; T. Bower, *Klaus Barbie*, pp. 243–5; E. Paris, *L'affaire Barbie*, pp. 164–248; J. Givet, *Le cas vergès* (Editions Lieu Commun, Paris, 1986).

26 Les éditions de Minuit, Paris, 1968.

27 *De la stratégie judiciaire*, p. 183.

28 Ibid., p. 104.

29 Ibid., p. 103.

30 Ibid., pp. 165–6.

31 Ibid., p. 168.

32 Ibid., p. 175.

33 Cf. E. Paris, *L'affaire Barbie*, p. 225.

34 H. Arendt, *Eichmann in Jerusalem*, p. 287.

8 Abraham and Antigone: Two Conflicting Imperatives

1 In 1944, German troops commanded by Colonel Walter Reder massacred all the inhabitants of the small Italian village of Marzabotto, in the province of Bologna. Most of the 1,836 killed were women and children. The military action was carried out by way of reprisal for the attacks of partisans in the area. According to some eyewitness accounts, two members of the German troops refused to take part in the shooting of harmless civilians, and were executed by order of Colonel Reder.

2 Genesis, 22, 1–12.

3 S. Milgram, *Obedience to Authority* (Yale University Press, New Haven, 1974).

4 S. Milgram, 'Some conditions of obedience and disobedience to authority', *Human Relations* 18 (1965), p. 75.

5 A. V. Dicey, *Introduction to the Study of Law of the Constitution*,

10th edn. (Macmillan, London, 1959), p. 303.

6   The decision in the *Wirz* case is reprinted in L. Friedman, *The Law of War*, vol. I (Random House, New York 1972), p. 783ff. The passage reported in my text is at p. 796.

On the appalling conditions of prisoners at Andersonville, see J. McElroy, *Andersonville: a Story of Rebel Military Prisons* (1895), (Fawcett, New York, 1962).

7   B. V. A. Röling, 'The significance of the laws of war', quoted above (n.17 of essay on Hiroshima and Nagasaki), pp. 137–9.

8   On the *Brussels* case, see J. W. Garner, *International Law and the World War*, vol. 1 (Longmans, Green, London, 1920), pp. 407–13.

9   For the English text of the decisions in the *Dover Castle* and *Llandovery Castle* cases, see *American Journal of International Law*, 16 (1922), pp. 704–8 and 708–24 respectively.

10 *Trial of the Major War Criminals before the International Military Tribunal, Nuremberg 14 November 1945–1 October 1946* (Nuremberg, 1947), vol. I, p. 248.

11 H. Arendt, *Eichmann in Jerusalem: a Report on the Banality of Evil* (Penguin Books, London, 1976), p. 253ff.

12 *Trial of the Major War Criminals*, vol. 18, p. 6 (final plea of defendant Keitel, by Nelte).

13 *Trial of the Major War Criminals*, vol. I, p. 226.

14 Ibid., p. 223.

15 Ibid., p. 224.

16 For the text of the decision in the *Einsatzgruppen* case, see *Annual Digest and Reports of Public International Law Cases* 15 (1948) [London, 1953], pp. 656–68.

17 For the text of the decision see L. Friedman, *The Law of War*, vol. II, p. 1421ff. (the passage quoted above is at p. 1431).

18 These words were written by Goebbels on 28 May 1944 in an article in the German periodical *Völkischer Beobachter*. The article was intended to justify the murder of Allied pilots by German mobs. Goebbels contended that 'the pilots cannot validly claim that as soldiers they obeyed orders', and then went on to write the words quoted above in my text. The whole passage of Goebbels' article was quoted at Nuremberg by the French Chief Prosecutor François de Menthon: see, *Trial of the Major War Criminals*, vol. 5, p. 418.

19 See *Law Reports of Trials of War Criminals, selected and prepared by the UN War Crimes Commission* (1947–9), vol. I, p. 1ff (the passage I have quoted is at p. 12).

20 See *International Law Reports*, vol. 36, pp. 277–342. The passages quoted are at pp. 315 and 339, respectively.

21 See *Handbuch Militärisches Grundwissen*, 5th edn (Militärverlag der DDR, Berlin, 1972), p. 61 (section 5.3.4).

22 For the statement of the US Judge advocate in the *Calley* case see L.

Friedman, *The Law of War*, vol. II, p. 1703ff; the statement in the *Medina* case is pp. 1279ff. The decision handed down by the Court of Military Appeals in the Calley case is reprinted in *International Lawyer* 8 (1974), p. 523ff.

An account of the trial before the Court Martial is given by R. Hammer, *The Court-Martial of Lt. Calley* (Coward and McCann, New York, 1971). On the follow-up to the trial, see *International Herald Tribune*, 22–3 December 1973; *New York Times*, 26 September 1974.

23 T. Taylor, in L. Friedman, *The Law of War*, vol. I, p. XXIV.

24 See *International Herald Tribune*, 2–3 February 1974.

25 For the drafting documents of the Genocide Convention on the question at issue, see *Ad hoc Committee on Genocide, Summary Records*, Un docs E/AC.25/SR.18. See also *General Assembly Official Records*, 3rd Session, part. I, VIth Committee, pp. 302–14.

26 UN doc. E/AC.25/SR.28 (10 May 1948), p. 9.

27 Y. Dinstein, *The Defense of 'Obedience to Superior Orders' in International Law* (Sijthoff, Leyden, 1965), p. 219.

28 See Diplomatic Conference on Humanitarian Law, *Official Records*, vol. IX, p. 27ff.

29 *Official Records*, vol. IX, p. 143 (doc. CDDH/I/SR.52, para. 38).

30 F. Bacon, *Novum Organum*. 1, 78. (*Sunt enim non minus temporum quam regionum eremi et vastitates.*)

31 J.-J. Rousseau, *Discours sur l'origine et les fondements de l'inégalité parmi les hommes* (Gallimard, Paris, 1965), p. 19.

9 Front Line National Judges and International Law

1 *House of Lords* (1938), AC 485. The text of the decision is almost completely reprinted in *Annual Digest and Reports of Public International Law Cases 1938–1940* (Butterworth, London, 1942), p. 250ff. The passage I quote is at p. 254.

2 For the decision of the Rome Tribunal of 28 November 1968, see *Rivista di dir. internazionale privato e processuale*, vol. 5, 1969, p. 797ff; the decision of the Court of Cassation of 30 September 1968 is p. 246ff. For the final agreement between Italy and Japan see *Rivista di dir. internazionale*, vol. 59, 1976, p. 166 (cf. also pp. 230–1).

3 The best account of the McLeod case is given by R. Jennings, 'The Caroline and McLeod Case', *American Journal of International Law* 32 (1938), p. 82ff.

4 Later on 22 September 1985, the French Prime Minister L. Fabius publicly admitted that the French agents who had sunk the *Rainbow Warrior* had acted at the orders of French authorities. See J. Charpentier, 'L'affaire du *Rainbow Warrior*', *Annuaire Francais de*

droit international 31 (1985), pp. 210–20. See also G. Apollis, 'Le reglement de l'affaire du "Rainbow Warrior"', *Revue generale de droit international public*, 91 (1987), pp. 9ff.

5 For the English text of the decision see *The Japanese Annual of International Law* 8 (1964), p. 212ff. The passage I quote is at p. 250.

6 For this case, see first of all the *Memorandum for the US submitted to the Court of Appeals for the Second Circuit in Filartiga v. Pena-Irala*, in *International Legal Materials* 3 (1980), p. 585ff. The decision of the Court of Appeals of the Second Circuit (no. 191, Docket 79–6090) is in 630 *Federal Reporter* 2nd Series 876 (Ed Cir. 1980). As for the facts of the case, I have heavily drawn upon R. P. Claude, 'The case of Joelito Filartiga and the Clinic of Hope', *Human Rights Quarterly* 5 (1983), p. 275ff.

On the Filartiga case and its effects, see among other authors: J. M. Blum and R. G. Steinhardt, 'Federal jurisdiction over international human rights claims: the Alien Tort Claims Act after Filartiga v. Pena Irala', *Harvard International Law Journal* 22, 1981, p. 53ff. J. Hadley Louden, 'The domestic application of international human rights law: evolving the species', *Hastings International and Comparative Law Review* 5, 1983, p. 177ff; A. P. Della Pietra Jr, 'Limiting the scope of federal jurisdiction under the Alien Tort Statute', *Virginia Journal of International Law* 24 (1984), p. 941ff.

7 See 168 US 250, 18 Supreme Court 83; the most important part of the decision is reprinted in J.B. Moore, *A Digest of International Law* (Washington, 1906), vol. II, p. 33ff.

8 See US Court of Appeals, paras 13–14.

9 See *Dreyfus* v. *von Fink*, in 534 *Federal Reporter* 2nd Series 24, at p. 31 (decision of the Court of Appeals of the Second Circuit, 1976).

10 See the decision in the *Letelier* case in *International Law Reports* 63 (1982), p. 378ff.

11 I shall quote the *Siderman* case from the typewritten text (I do not know whether it has been published yet).

12 See the Note of the Embassy of Argentina to the State Department, of 16 February 1983, annexed to the letter of the State Department of 28 March 1983 to the US District Court, Central District of California.

13 See e.g. the *Hanoch Tel-Oren* case (726 *Federal Reporter*, 2nd Series, 774ff.) and the other cases quoted in the articles mentioned *supra*, in n.6. See also the workshop 'Jurisdiction in Human Rights Cases: is the *Tel-Oren* Case a Step Backward?', in *Proceedings of the American Society of International Law*, 1985, pp. 361ff.

Index